Wise Mind, Open Mind is an outstanding guidebook to applying mindfulness practices to artfully navigate times of change and crisis. Alexander has offered his mind, heart, and soul to illuminate strategies that release destructive beliefs and help readers find more creativity, insight, and flow. A seasoned, loving psychologist, Alexander combines spirituality with gems from his clinical practice in a wonderful contribution to the healing arts.

—Judith Orloff, MD, author of *Emotional Freedom*

In Wise Mind, Open Mind, *readers will learn how weaving mindfulness and contemporary psychology can heal, enliven, and free their spirits. Ronald Alexander's three-step process highlights key elements to help readers untangle emotional knots and discover the love and clarity that is our deepest nature. This book is a lucid and inspiring guide on the spiritual path!*

—Tara Brach, Ph.D., founder of Insight Meditation Community of Washington, DC, author of *Radical Acceptance*

This book contains very sound and creative clinical advice to those trying to change their lives. Alexander melds positive thinking psychology, highly regarded as a major element in personal change, with ideas from a variety of meditative traditions drawn from more than thirty years of experience. This man lives and practices what he says. The book will change your life if you let it.

—Stuart W. Twemlow, MD, professor of psychiatry and behavioral sciences at Baylor College of Medicine in Houston, TX

Alexander has done a superb job of making the deep and complex principles of Buddhism and mindfulness practical and available to help people make profound shifts in their lives. There are many recent books based in mindfulness, but Alexander has been immersed in the practice of mindfulness for decades. Beware: this book could have serious side effects of happiness and peace.

—Bill O'Hanlon, author of *Pathways to Spirituality* and *Do One Thing Different*

Wise Mind, Open Mind *weaves a brilliant tapestry of many valuable and insightful ideas. Alexander's methods integrate contemporary positive psychology, creativity thinking, Buddhist psychology, and mindfulness practices. His book is a step-by-step practical guide for anyone who is undergoing life changes or crisis. Following Alexander's model can help to facilitate inner transformation and bring forth new possibilities for change. A wonderful read for one seeking a new path towards healing!*

—Marion Solomon, Ph.D., faculty member at University of California, Los Angeles

"We have the creativity in us that creates the universe—all we need do is be aware of it. This book provides a wise road map to the treasure within."
—Ram Dass, author of *Remember, Be Here Now*

In Wise Mind, Open Mind, *Alexander presents a mindful approach to navigating crisis that serves to help us better understand ourselves and recognize our hidden potential. His three-step process allows us to dissolve any resistance to change, immerse ourselves in the present, and eventually emerge strengthened, renewed, and with a deeper sense of purpose.*
—Alberto Villoldo, Ph.D., author of *Shaman, Healer, Sage* and *Courageous Dreaming*

Fusing Western psychology and Buddhist practices, this book provides clear guidance and instruction and helps us to transform our thinking. It is both informative and greatly supportive.
—Sharon Salzberg, author of *Lovingkindness*

Creativity often arises either from inner disturbance or from great peace. In this book, a culmination of thirty years of insight from his practice, Alexander explores the latter method—the flashes of genius that flow from the silence of the heart.
—Catherine Ingram, author of *In the Footsteps of Gandhi, Passionate Presence,* and *A Crack in Everything*

Alexander offers practical tools to navigate the dark waters of our unconscious resistances to the tides of change with the clear, compassionate, fierce wisdom of a sage. He speaks to our deepest fears, doubts, and desires like an old friend. Every page gives real, transforming insight, written with profound depth by one of the best East-West embodied teachers and psychotherapists in the world. A treasure for all of us in these times of change.
—Shiva Rea, MA, yogini at Samudra Global School for Living Yoga

France is the birthplace of hypnosis, and Freud made it the cradle of psychoanalysis. Then Milton Erickson created another revolution. Alexander offers yet another opening, an opening of the mind and of the heart, which made me open my eyes wide. There is no point in describing the taste of a mango; you have to sink your teeth into it, and I suggest we do the same with this book.
—Olivier Perrot, psychologist and president of the Association Française de Nouvelle Hypnose (French Association for New Hypnosis)

WISE MIND | OPEN MIND

finding
purpose & meaning
in times of
crisis, loss & change

RONALD A. ALEXANDER, PH.D.

NEW HARBINGER PUBLICATIONS, INC.

Publisher's Note

Distributed in Canada by Raincoast Books

Copyright © 2008 by Ronald A. Alexander
New Harbinger Publications, Inc.
5674 Shattuck Avenue
Oakland, CA 94609
www.newharbinger.com

Excerpt from "Poetry" from ISLA NEGRA by Pablo Neruda, translated by Alastair Reid. Translation copyright © 1981 by Alastair Reid. Reprinted by permission of Farrar, Straus and Giroux, LLC.

Pablo Neruda. Fragment from "La Poesía", ISLA NEGRA ©Fundación Pablo Neruda, 2009.

"The Song of a Man Who Has Come Through" by D. H. Lawrence, from THE COMPLETE POEMS OF D. H. LAWRENCE by D. H. Lawrence, edited by V. de Sola Pinto & F. W. Roberts, copyright © 1964, 1971 by Angelo Ravagli and C. M. Weekly, Executors of the Estate of Frieda Lawrence Ravagli. Used by permission of Viking Penguin, a division of Penguin Group (USA) Inc.

From *The Way of the Bodhisattva*, by Shantideva; translated by the Padmakara Translation Group, ©1997, 2006 by the Padmakara Translation Group. Reprinted by arrangement with Shambhala Publications Inc., Boston, MA. www.shambhala.com.

From *Book of Longing*, copyright 2006 by Leonard Cohen. Reprinted by permission of HarperCollins Publishers, 57. Originally published in the United States by Ecco, an imprint of HarperCollins Publishers.

Quote from "Statue of Buddha" reprinted with permission from Many Rivers Press, *Fire in the Earth* (Langley, WA: Many Rivers Press, 1992), 85. www.davidwhyte.com.

Excerpt from *The Scheme of Things*, copyright 1980 by Allen B. Wheelis. Reprinted by permission of Houghton Mifflin Harcourt Publishing Company.

Angeles Arrien as quoted in *The Millionth Circle: How to Change Ourselves and the World—The Essential Guide to Women's Circles* by Jean Shinoda Bolen (Conari Press, 1999). Reprinted with permission of Angeles Arrien.

Quote "Dove that ventured outside", translated by Stephen Mitchell, from *The Selected Poetry of Rainer Maria Rilke* by Rainer Maria Rilke, translated by Stephen Mitchell, translation copyright © 1980, 1981, 1982 Stephen Mitchell. Used by permission of Random House, Inc.

All Rights Reserved
Printed in the United States of America

Acquired by Tesilya Hanauer; Cover design by Amy Shoup; Edited by Nelda Street

Library of Congress Cataloging-in-Publication Data on file
Alexander, Ronald A.
  Wise mind, open mind : finding purpose and meaning in times of crisis, loss, and change / Ronald A. Alexander.
    p. cm.
  Includes bibliographical references.
  ISBN-13: 978-1-57224-643-0 (pbk. : alk. paper)
  ISBN-10: 1-57224-643-X (pbk. : alk. paper) 1. Self-actualization (Psychology) 2. Centering (Psychology) 3. Mindfulness-based cognitive therapy. I. Title.
  BF637.S4A572 2009
  158.1--dc22

                    2009023474

11 10 09   10 9 8 7 6 5 4 3 2 1   First printing

Contents

Foreword

Long ago, I wrote that there's a great spiritual hunger in this land. How true is this now, in these times of economic crisis and environmental upheaval? Many are looking deeper for satisfaction and fulfillment, having discovered that material and technological progress—valuable as it may be—still leaves us wanting. Throughout history, people have turned inward, looking for inner freedom and genuine creativity, and the transformative power that tends to follow behind its exercise. Milarepa sang his thousands of extemporaneous songs of enlightenment outside his Himalayan cave; later, they were memorized and eventually written down by his disciples. Han Shan inscribed his poems on the rocks and trees of Cold Mountain, while Li Po folded many of his handwritten poems into paper boats and set them asail on river waters. In his own way, each of these inspirational figures transformed his experience of the world into a medium that could be intimately and immediately shared, a creative process in the service of wisdom, compassionate action, and liberation, both individual and collective.

As Ron Alexander points out in *Wise Mind, Open Mind,* the travails of pain and suffering, adversity, loss, and change are not optional in this life, but the way we relate to these things is certainly within our control. We cannot control the winds of karma, but we can learn to sail and navigate better, becoming masters rather than victims of our fate. The potential for creative transformation lies within all of us. Some give this potential free rein in their lives. For them, the inevitable flux of experience becomes a potent fuel for the fostering of beauty and joyous, buoyant clarity. Others resist this inner potential, or even fear the freedom that comes from such autonomy. For them, change is at best distressing, at worst a horror.

The cause of suffering is clinging, attachment, greed, desire, resistance, fixation—call it whatever you like. It is often called craving or overweening desire. The word literally is *tanha* in Pali (*samudaya* in Sanskrit), which suggests thirst. Because we crave, continually desire and thirst for various experiences and things, and because created things are never ultimately satisfying, we suffer. That's where the chain of suffering can be addressed: whether or not we cling to things and crave experiences. It's not that we have to get rid of the things themselves. Things are not the problem. It is the attachment—the identification with things—that causes suffering. Tilopa wrote, "It is not outer objects which entangle us. It is inner clinging which entangles us." It's not what happens to us but what we make of it that makes all the difference. Here is the secret of mastery.

This book will introduce you to some practice traditions that can start you off on the process of calming and refining your spiritual awareness and recognizing the true nature of your own mind and heart, of allowing a path so creativity may emerge when life takes its inevitable twists and turns, of loosening the vise-like grip we have on the world—a hold that keeps us fettered. Here is a lucid, practical guide to beginning a mindfulness practice, which helps us to be more fully present, intentional, and engaged. It offers simple ways to let go of destructive beliefs, unwholesome judgments, and the persistent need to feel in control. The book is a kind invitation to open your mind to the richness of experience and the profound power you have within yourself to foster happiness and wisdom in your life.

I welcome you, then, to this journey of exploration and discovery. In Ron Alexander, you've found a capable and friendly guide. Paraphrasing the title of the fourth part of *Wise Mind, Open Mind,* I wish you smooth sailing and a blissful passage as you set out into the unknown with trust, faith, and joyful enthusiasm.

—Lama Surya Das
Dzogchen Center
Cambridge, Massachusetts
June 2009

Acknowledgments

I wish to thank the following individuals for their help in birthing this book: Nancy Peske, for bringing out the expression of my ideas through her extraordinary skills in editing, simplicity, and organization, a combination without which this book wouldn't have been possible; Catharine Sutker, acquisitions editor, for bringing me to New Harbinger and for loving this book, Jess Beebe and Nelda Street for their editing skills, and all the other folks at New Harbinger; Jilisa Snyder, Ph.D., for her invaluable feedback as an outside reader; Lama Surya Das for his kindness and Buddha generosity in writing the foreword to this book; Scott Edelstein, my fabulous literary attorney, a constant source of advice and reflection; Robert Gurette, MD, for bringing me to New England Educational Institute to offer my teachings and assisting to shape my skills as a speaker with detailed persistence; Jeffrey Hutter, Ph.D., my co-teacher at UCLA Extension, who made it possible for us to offer Zen and mindfulness programs at the university over the past thirty years, as well as Marion Solomon, Ph.D., for her inspiration and encouragement to write and her innovation in bringing to UCLA the Conference on Mindfulness and Psychotherapy; and all of the faculty, students, and administrators at Pacifica Graduate Institute, Pepperdine University, and Ryokan College.

I would like to thank my writer's wisdom council of support for their wisdom, creativity, and inspiration all along the way: Joel Belsky, Ann Maria Dunne, Pamela Fields, Ph.D., Bill O'Hanlon, M.A., Catherine Ingram, Carl Kugel, MA, Jay Levin, MA (founder of *LA Weekly*), Judith

Orloff, MD, Charlotte Resnick, Ph.D., Sebastian Lampe, MS, and especially Alberto Villoldo, Ph.D., for his friendship and guidance with this project.

I would also like to thank Tara Brach, Ph.D.; Daniel P. Brown, Ph.D.; Jim Blechman, MD; Karen Bohan, MA; **Georgina Cannon, M.NLP;** Jim Clancy, MA; Michael Conforti, Ph.D.; Ram Dass; Vera Dunn, Ph.D.; Ken Dychtwald, Ph.D.; Milton Erickson, MD; Suzanne Evans; Rhonda Gibson; Susan Golant, MA; Elisabeth Halfpapp; John Heider, Ph.D.; Elisabeth Hoffmeister, Diplom.; Derek Ireland; Stephen Johnson, Ph.D.; Anita Jung, MS; Sandy Levine; Jenny Boyd-Levitt, Ph.D., for an a up-close glimpse of the magical musical creative; Teri Lindeman, MA; Alan Meskil, Ph.D.; Carol Meskil, MA; Lisa Morcolli-Latham for her creative eye and her work behind the camera; Rasmani Deborah Orth, Ed.D.; Erving Polster, Ph.D.; Marjorie L. Rand, Ph.D.; Shiva Rea, MA; Jeffrey Trop, MD; Tsoknyi Rinpoche; Stuart Twemlow, MD, Ph.D.; Sharon Salzberg; Estelle Shane, Ph.D.; Jeni Tyson, Ph.D.; David Van Nuys, Ph.D.; Gordon Wheeler, Ph.D.; and a special note of appreciation to Nancy Lunney-Wheeler, MA, at Esalen Institute, who saw my potential.

Thanks to all my patients, students, and trainees, who've taught me so much; to my three wonderful assistants, who've labored with my notes and graphs throughout the years: Rhonda Bryant, Diane Carter, and Debra Yates; and to Dana Felice, for her excellent effort, focus, efficiency, and divine inspiration. To all of my teachers, guides, and friends who assisted me in opening the doors of perception, I am forever thankful and filled with your grace.

INTRODUCTION

Creativity, Mindfulness, and Change

Wake up.
Life is transient,
Swiftly passing.
Be aware of the great matter.
Don't waste time.

—Buddhist proverb

As a young man growing up in Boston in the zeitgeist of the late 1960s, I spent much of my time in Cambridge's Harvard Square, where tattered paperbacks on Zen Buddhism and existential philosophy were commonly seen in the hands of students and professors alike. Cambridge also seemed a natural hub for many of the great musicians of the era, including Bob Dylan, Joan Baez, Tom Rush, The Band, Joni Mitchell, Simon and Garfunkel, and the Byrds, and it was the place where the British bands first landed and rehearsed for their national tours. The Beatles, the Rolling Stones, the Who, Led Zeppelin, Van Morrison, and Donovan played the local clubs, from Boston's Psychedelic Supermarket to the Harvard Bowl or the Boston Garden. Like many of my peers, I bought a folk guitar, joined a local band, and imagined that my music would change the world.

The connection between creativity and transformation intrigued me. I was fascinated to see so many people around me opening themselves up to new influences and new ways of thinking, transforming not just their art but also themselves. Instead of simply accepting the status quo, they began to question their beliefs and habits. Around the world, it seemed as if people were awakening from a deep sleep. I, too, awakened and became swept up in the winds of a cultural and spiritual revolution that carried ideas from east to west.

I felt inspired to study psychology and Buddhism at the University of Massachusetts, Amherst; California State University, Sonoma; and the Humanistic Psychology Institute, and, in 1976, began my career as a psychotherapist. In my first year of private practice, I founded the Center for Health and Healing at Cedars-Sinai Medical Center in Los Angeles, and soon was treating a flurry of creative clients, ranging from writers, painters, directors, producers, actors, and musicians to executives in development, marketing, advertising, and promotion within the television, film, and music industries. I found I was able to speak their language: the language of the creative process. Working with them helped me hone my ideas about how to use mindfulness and creativity to deal with unexpected changes and to break out of stagnation. Soon, I began teaching and leading workshops on the creative process of change, helping people explore what sparks an interest in change and why it's often difficult for people and organizations to transform themselves.

I believe that within all of us lies dormant the potential for tremendous transformation that can lead to great happiness. In my graduate work in counseling psychology and, over the years, in my private practice as a mind-body psychotherapist; educator; trainer; and consultant to the Cottonwood Recovery centers in Tucson and London and to many hospitals, clinics, and educational and therapeutic centers throughout the United States, I've helped thousands of individuals and companies set off on their own artistic journeys and reinvent themselves. I've watched clients let go of their false beliefs about who they are and what roads are open to them, and observed them as they found new paths to fulfillment and happiness that were previously hidden by their fear of change. Cultivating mindfulness, they were able to begin seeing their lives as a canvas for self-expression that could, and should, reflect their personal passions and values. Even when their lives shifted abruptly and caused them great suffering, they were able to feel their pain and allow it to dissipate as they let go of the past and attained what the Buddhists call *open-mind consciousness*. This is the creative state artists immerse themselves in, an almost magical state of being in which you can tune in to the unconscious and even the collective unconscious, emerging with fresh and original ideas, passion, and inspiration.

In writing this book, my goal is to create a unique opportunity for you to learn methods and techniques drawn from the ancient schools of Buddhist mindfulness meditation and the current field of positive psychology so that you can foster your own transformation, become more at ease with the process of change, and view transition as positive and exciting. Just as a painter's heart begins to beat faster as the paintbrush takes him to places he hadn't imagined going, or a photographer discovers an extraordinary texture in an everyday object, when you attain the state of awareness known as *open mind*, you'll discover myriad possibilities for your life. *Wise Mind, Open Mind* will teach you the all-important three-step process anyone can use to navigate change:

1. *Let go* of resistance.

2. *Tune in* to your creative unconscious, experiencing open mind.

3. *Move forward* with a practical plan for transformation.

Whether you know you're ready to change or sense that you should, whether you're struggling to accept that your circumstances have shifted or you're feeling stuck or blocked by an unknown force and unable to move forward, it's important to recognize that change is unavoidable. Life is continually in flux, and even that which seems immutable can be destroyed or altered in an instant. The Buddhists refer to this as the *law of impermanence*. Nothing stays the same, not even the rocks and the mountains, which rain, snow, and rivers sculpt over time. Each day, millions of your body's cells die while millions more are born. Stasis is an illusion our egos create to fend off the fear of change.

When change is not your choice, you can't avoid suffering, but you can choose to view the change as an avenue to personal evolution. You can push aside your perceived limitations and let go of the habits that have provided you with comfort, familiarity, and a false sense of safety, and go forth with fear in check, using creativity to illuminate new paths.

You can break out of the dynamic of push and pull, of desire for change and resistance to it, and step past the boundaries of the known. You can recognize that while you may attain some comfort from the habit of trying to control the flow of your life, clinging to the familiar also breeds boredom and discontent. It prevents you from fully inhabiting your life and keeps you mired in regret. It keeps you small.

The secret to successful reinvention is knowing that you don't have to greet change with apprehension and resistance, focusing on the potential for suffering, because if you take that route, you experience the very suffering you'd hoped to avoid. When it's time for change, whether you're losing a loved one, your perfect health, the job you loved, or the lifestyle you enjoyed, you have the opportunity to make your life even better than it is, as unfathomable as that may seem at first.

Whatever your vocation, you, like all people, are an artist, and your masterpiece is your own life. In my many years as a therapist, I've found that most people wish they could be an actor, painter, singer, or other type of artist, and I encourage them to find ways to express themselves in the arts, because I believe that all creativity is vitalizing. However, I tell my clients that they don't have to be Mick Jagger to be a performer or Andy Warhol to be a painter, and in fact, even if they never sing a note or pick up a paintbrush, they can be artists of their own lives. Artistic aspirations are often a metaphor for the desire to live more creatively and authentically, according to the dreams of the soul instead of the expectations of society. We admire the great artists, because they have the ability to tune in to their inner passions and give birth to beauty, only to reinvent themselves again and again. Their mastery of the art of creative transformation inspires us.

But any of us, no matter what we do or how we define ourselves, can master this art. Artistic expression can take many forms, from playing guitar in a rock-and-roll band to parenting in a fresh and original way. I have a physician whose approach to interacting with patients is very different: When he asks how you are, he genuinely listens to the answer; if you mention that you're feeling emotional pain, he empathizes by telling you about something that caused him emotional pain; and if you say you have a physical ailment, he often says, "I wonder what your soul is telling you." His approach is creative and authentic, because he has a passion for healing.

I also have a financial-planner client who's in touch with his own passion and creativity, and very happy in his work. For many years, he was a film director whose animated short films were shown at film festivals around the world, but he discovered that he truly loves investing. He has crafted a life as a financial advisor who truly listens to the needs of his clients and helps them invest their money in ways that are meaningful to them. He guides people in becoming mindful of their feelings about risk and security, and in doing so, he inspires them to be more self-aware in other areas. Financial planning, working with numbers and helping people make money, is merely the vehicle for assisting his clients in exploring and discovering what they most want for themselves and in transforming the quality of their lives. Where once his interactions felt boring and businesslike to him, now he's enthusiastic about talking to his clients. That attitude affects them as well, because they leave his office feeling infused with excitement about how they can use their money and investments to meet their personal goals.

When you tune in to the endless source of creativity that's available to you in open mind, and honor your passion, you live the life of an artist. But to master the art of creative transformation and construct a new vision for your life, you must accept that there are no shortcuts and no formulas for avoiding discomfort and suffering. Simply wishing and believing that you can attract what you desire, or putting your head down and working harder at what you're already doing, hinders the process, blocking the flow of ideas and possibilities. The secret to crafting a new life that's fulfilling and in alignment with your deepest values is twofold:

1.   Develop a mindfulness practice.

2.   Immerse yourself in the three-step art of creative transformation whenever you're faced with crisis or a stagnant situation that you know must be changed, refreshed, and enlivened.

You can master both of these techniques and use them to help yourself move out of suffering and into the next chapter in your life.

PART I

Preparing for Creative Transformation

CHAPTER 1

The Three Steps to Creating a Mandala for Your Life

You see things, and you say "Why?"
But I dream things that never were, and I say, "Why not?"

—George Bernard Shaw

In Buddhism, a *mandala* is a beautiful, intricate, circular sand painting of many colors that depicts the relationships among the celestial bodies in the cosmos and represents the turning of the wheel of fortune. Jungians say a mandala can be a depiction of the parts of the self, united in harmony and balance. It's an exquisite symbol that visually renders the cycle of life, from birth to death to birth again. Yet, after spending countless hours creating this work of art, the one who has designed it and meticulously laid the colored sand will sweep it away, obliterating the carefully constructed lines. As the image of the mandala fades into memory, its creator reflects on the impermanent nature of everything we experience.

When dramatic shifts occur in our lives, we can become nearly paralyzed with fear, anger, grief, and resentment. We enter a state of shock and forget that with loss comes rebirth. On some level, we understand that we must design a new life, a new mandala, but we struggle between trying to figure out what we want to do next and being overwhelmed by the intense emotions associated with loss. Clinging to the past, we resist the opportunity to embrace the creative process that requires us to let go of the mind's limited way of thinking about ourselves and the situation at hand. But if we can find the courage to enter this process, to experience the state of consciousness Buddhists call "open mind," accessing our deepest, or core, creativity, we can begin to tune in to what we most want for ourselves. You can ensure that your new life is in sync with your deepest values. You can let go of your attachments to what was and what you thought would be. You can choose to let go of fear and trust that a palette of many colors, some of which you may never have seen before, will be available for creating a new mandala: a new life of beauty that's in harmony with the song of the soul.

A Creative Transformation After Tragedy

A few years ago, a couple named Mark and Selena came to me on the advice of friends, asking me to be their therapist and help them cope with the most devastating of losses: their two young children had been killed in a car crash when their teenage babysitter, who was driving, took her eyes off the road, crossed the centerline, and caused a head-on collision at sixty miles an hour. The babysitter had somehow survived, but Mark and Selena were overwhelmed with guilt, anger, and feelings of loss. They could barely function and couldn't begin to imagine how they could go on without their children or why they would want to. Although they couldn't have anticipated the accident that took their children's lives, they still felt crippling guilt, profound sorrow, and bottomless grief. They revisited that fatal day over and over again in their minds, obsessing about what might've been if they hadn't left the children in the babysitter's care. Only the repeated urgings of their closest friends brought them to my office to begin to work through their suffering.

I counseled them for several months and taught them to use the program in this book, which requires cultivating a mindfulness meditation practice and undergoing the three-step art of creative transformation. I knew that to help them begin healing, I needed to guide them in letting go of their resistance to this change that had been forced upon them so dramatically. Understandably, they felt no desire to move forward with their lives, so our initial healing work focused simply on the first step of *letting go*. Both Mark and Selena had to give up their feelings of guilt and the unconscious belief that if they were to enjoy life again and make new plans for themselves, they would be bad parents, betraying their children. To help them stop embracing this belief that kept them focused on their loss, I explored with them what their children would say to them if they could have one more conversation. Mark and Selena recognized that their son and daughter would tell them to continue living, rather than compound the tragedy by sleepwalking through life and feeling too guilty and afraid to move forward.

I also taught them practices to fully experience their grief and be mindful of the moments in the day when they could feel positive and focused on what was happening in the present. Only when they fully embraced this step of letting go—of the past, their guilt, and the old dream of watching their two children grow up—could they begin to take the second step in the art of creative transformation: *tuning in*.

When faced with the question, "And now what?" most of us are less likely to find the answer among our thoughts than if we were to enter open-mind consciousness. Open mind is a state of creativity that's very familiar to artists, one that all of us experienced as playful children but many of us have forgotten about. Also known as "the field of possibilities," "the creative void," and even "the creative soup," it's the state of awareness in which we feel a sense of timelessness, openness, and unlimited possibilities. It's the source of the most authentic and original concepts, which spring forth naturally and spontaneously. In this state, we can begin to imagine situations and opportunities that would never occur to us in our ordinary consciousness.

As Mark and Selena's therapist, I knew that I could use the usual clinical methods to try to help them continue the healing process, but clearly, it could take several years before they would be ready to move out of their grief and begin to envision a new life. I decided to meditate on their situation, and in doing so, attained open mind. What came to me was the visual image of the subcontinent of India. "That's curious," I thought, but I sat with it rather than dismiss it as the product of an overactive mind. Soon, as if a voice had spoken to me, I had an inner knowing that I needed to suggest to Mark and Selena, who had conveyed an openness to the idea of traveling, to take several months off from their jobs and go to India—to a city called Varanasi. Varanasi is known as a holy place where the dying go to prepare for death and where bodies are prepared for the traditional cremation and return to the sacred Ganges River.

My logical, rational mind said, "Ron, that's crazy. Why would you send two grieving and suffering parents who have no spiritual connection to India, and who are Lutherans from the Midwest, to Varanasi, where they know no one and would see death and suffering all around them?"

Rather than talk myself out of what my intuition had told me, I discussed it with several of my colleagues, whom I think of as my wisdom council of support (see chapter 11). They come from a variety of therapeutic traditions, and all are thoughtful, wise professionals whom I knew would carefully consider what I was presenting and give me honest, helpful feedback. The verdict was unanimous: it was a terrible idea.

WISDOM COUNCIL OF SUPPORT

Your wisdom council of support consists of respected and trusted people in your life, whom you rely on for advice and creative ideas.

I took in their words and valued their opinions and insights, but in my mindfulness meditation practice each morning, I connected with my intuition, and it kept telling me the same thing: encourage Mark and Selena to go to Varanasi. Finally, one of my old teachers and mentors, Ram Dass, told me, "I think you may be on to something. They need to immerse themselves in their grief instead of denying it. Where better to do that than India?"

Mark, who was from a blue-collar background and had never traveled, and Selena, who distracted herself from her deep sadness by working long hours as an administrator at a nonprofit organization, had begun establishing a mindfulness meditation practice, as I'd instructed. They had begun to open up to the possibility of change but had no idea how to go about exiting their suffering and moving forward with their lives. Although they weren't sure how they would benefit from a trip to Varanasi, they meditated on it and told me that taking the trip felt "right" to them.

In India, Mark and Selena connected with their grief as they observed the dead and dying, but at the same time, they started to feel a sense of connection to other people and to a world in which suffering is inevitable. They didn't know the language and couldn't converse with most of the people they met, but their eyes expressed compassion toward parents who stood by the river, ready to undergo the sacred rites for their children who had died. Mark and Selena ended up spending a couple of weeks working with a committed humanitarian in her facility for the poor. She did not try to explain to Mark and Selena how they might handle their loss but instead invited them to join her in her everyday work of attending to the sick and dying.

When they returned to the States, Mark and Selena told me they had finally begun to heal. The deep compassion that had been awakened in them had eased their grief, and they felt they'd transformed from suffering parents who had lost their children to people who reached out to other suffering parents. They said they no longer felt quite so alone.

Over the next few months, Mark and Selena continued their mindfulness meditation practice and began to immerse themselves in the state of open mind often. Selena, who had always loved music and had earned a fine arts degree but never pursued art as a career, tuned in to her own creativity, taking the second step in the three-step process of creative transformation. She accessed her passion for playing piano and sharing her music with others. Selena soon returned to school to earn a master's degree, and began to envision herself working with children as a music therapist.

Mark went back to his work as an electrician, but he now approached it in a very different way. His compassion had been awakened by his terrible suffering, and his time in India had inspired in him a sense that he had more to offer than simply repairing what was broken and doing whatever work his customers requested. Now, when he spoke to his clients about the work they wanted done on their homes, he suggested bold changes they hadn't considered. He pointed out ways they could change the lighting in their homes to create a feeling of spaciousness or comfort and calm. He listened closely to their plans, asking them how they wanted to use their space and making suggestions for how he might rewire a particular room to better suit their vision rather than simply do what they'd asked. When he worked with a couple who were renovating their home now that their last child had left for college, Mark was able to be patient and compassionate as he dealt with their ever-vacillating decisions, recognizing that they were still coming to terms with the difficult transition of no longer sharing their space with their son.

Selena began to work as a music therapist, and as she got to know her students, many of whom had special needs, her heart began to open to the idea of being a parent again. In time, Mark and Selena adopted two special-needs children and had another child of their own. They continue to talk about their children who died and keep photographs of them in their home, but they've now completed the third step in the art of creative transformation, *moving forward* into a new life and a new mandala.

MINDFULNESS

Mindfulness is an idea from Buddhism that's central to meditation, but it's also a way of life and a crucial tool in the art of creative transformation. You don't just meditate to become aware of your breathing, the sounds around you, your bodily sensations, or the existence of your core self that's not harried by an endless stream of thoughts. You establish a practice of meditation in order to develop the habit of mindfulness so that your awareness remains engaged when you leave the meditation cushion and go out into the world. You're able to act consciously instead of unconsciously. Developing mindfulness allows you to quickly and naturally become aware of what's really going on in any situation instead of being distracted by your thoughts, feelings, and actions or resisting the truth in order to avoid suffering.

Mindfulness allows you to hear the quiet inner voice that says "India," "wait," "forgive," "open," "music teacher," and "partnership" or to see images that make you stop and wonder about new possibilities you hadn't considered. You may have had a recurring dream with a symbol that appeared to you night after night until you finally took the time to contemplate what it meant, listened to its message, and chose a new course of action. With regular mindfulness practice, such symbols and messages will come to you when you're ready to receive them and act on them. But to practice mindfulness, you must develop the habit of gently pushing aside your distractions instead of allowing them to pull you in every direction.

At any given moment, you're probably focused on one thing—your thoughts, your emotions, or the task at hand—and brushing aside distractions as well as you can. If you're like most people, you often become extremely distracted by myriad sensations, feelings, and thoughts that drag you away from the inner self and its wisdom. You hear conflicting opinions, feel anxiety about the changes in your life, and focus your thoughts on mundane tasks such as fixing dinner or making phone calls.

Too often, our lives become all about our distractions, and in quiet moments, the thought occurs to us that we're not living authentically, in alignment with our deepest desires. Instead of a mandala, we have piles of colored sand that we push around aimlessly, creating and destroying these piles and yet never forming the beautiful, whole picture we long for.

Some of us have an inkling of what we'd like to create but are unaware of it most of the time because of our distractions, and some of us have no vision at all. With mindfulness, we can begin to quiet what the Buddhists call the "monkey mind," the chattering self that, like an untrained monkey roaming about a house alone, wreaking havoc and causing mischief, relentlessly generates distracting thoughts. When the monkey has been put back into his cage, we can begin the process of tuning in to the creativity deep inside of us.

> *Something knocked in my soul,*
> *fever or forgotten wings,*
> *and I made my own way,*
> *deciphering*
> *that fire,*
> *and I wrote the first, faint line,*
> *faint, without substance, pure*
> *nonsense, pure wisdom of someone who knows nothing;*
> *and suddenly I saw the heavens unfastened and open,*

—Pablo Neruda, "La Poesia"

THE THREE-STEP ART OF CREATIVE TRANSFORMATION

Creativity isn't something reserved for a special group of talented people, nor do you require a particular temperament to be creative. Whether you played an instrument in a garage band or never picked up a guitar, had a childhood dream of becoming a ballerina or imagined yourself in the NBA, or are a successful advertising director or an accountant, you can be a brilliant artist of life. You can open yourself up to the possibility of dramatic personal transformation by learning and using the three-step process of creative transformation available to all of us.

Unexpected change often provides the impetus to realize this tantalizing and exciting, yet frightening, potential. People like Al Gore, who found his road to the White House suddenly blocked and chose to focus on educating people about global warming, and Christopher Reeve, who left acting behind after becoming a quadriplegic and went on to become a film director and advocate for those suffering from spinal cord injuries, are objects of admiration for many, because they were able to let go of the past and transform their lives. In America, we've made pop-culture icons of figures from Jacqueline Kennedy to Bono, because they seem to epitomize the promise of self-reinvention. We long for just a fraction of the courage to move forward without looking back in sorrow and regret, but fear we don't have what it takes to rise from the ashes of our own loss.

The art of creative transformation is not about developing an "artistic temperament" or becoming a fine artist. It's a process for reinvention that you can use to free yourself from stagnation and steer the ship of self when the winds of change are blowing. When you begin to use this process, you stop feeling like the victim of circumstances and begin to see that you, too, can transform yourself and your life in a positive and exciting way.

Like a dream,
Whatever I enjoy
will become a memory;
the past is not revisited.

—Shantideva

Step 1: Let Go

The art of creative transformation begins with the willingness to be mindful of your hidden resistance, examine it, and break it down so that you can sweep it away like sand on a doorstep. If unwanted change has occurred, you're likely to become angry or upset, and struggle to regain what's been lost. You might find yourself closing your eyes to any other avenues available to you, and obsessing about the past and reclaiming what was once yours. This resistance blocks you from recognizing that what lies ahead for you might actually make you happier than you've ever been.

If all signs point to the need for change, it's important not to deny them and cling to the status quo even as it's slipping away. Many of us insist on staying in a relationship long after a partner has given up and moved on emotionally, or try to hold on to a job after the boss has encouraged us to take long lunches for interviews with other companies. In the first part of this book, I'll help you explore your own resistance to change and let go of all that's holding you back, so that you can be in open mind and accept, and even embrace, the impermanent nature of life.

Step 2: Tune In

The second step in the creative process is tuning in and listening to the wisdom of your soul by achieving open mind, the state in which core creativity takes place, beyond the limitations of the mind's thought processes. Whenever you reconnect to this core, authentic self through open mind, the temporary circumstances of life stop distracting you. You're able to trust that the creative process will produce opportunities and possibilities in due time. You don't find yourself feeling that you're running out of time and must make a decision quickly.

The soul, which recognizes its connection to the divine and to eternity, is quite different from your false, external self, the part of yourself that identifies with the temporary world of the senses. Your ego, or false self, will present you with a long list of arguments for fighting changes that you didn't ask for and avoiding changes that require you to break out of your comfort zone—even if the cost is your own happiness. In a panic, the ego will try to figure its way out of a crisis, but the soul never becomes anxious. It simply allows itself to be aware of your unique gifts, and provides the passion and creativity needed for you to reinvent yourself.

To master the art of change, you must stop identifying with this false self, which insists, "I can't," "I shouldn't," and "I'll never" and wants to replace what's lost with something that feels familiar. You must instead identify with the soul and its calling, a calling you can only hear in a state of open mind. Your brave, authentic self urges you to let go of your fears, take risks to live more deeply and fully, and take the leap to achieve your destiny. By accessing your soul, you'll unleash the driving force of your passions, and send yourself sailing into uncharted waters and climbing new mountains. Trust in this journey and know that when the fog of uncertainty parts, the way will be clear and you'll be exactly where you need to be.

Once you've developed the skill of attaining open mind, you'll begin to recognize what you most desire, because you won't be distracted by what your small, or *egoic*, mind, churns up. Your egoic mind is the small part of yourself that overly identifies with who you are as an individual. It's the aspect of your consciousness that has a sense of self-importance and is concerned with your desires and your place in the world. The egoic mind is incapable of perceiving that you are both an individual and a part of a greater, cosmic, interconnected self.

In open mind, you're freed of the limitations of your egoic mind so that you can begin to imagine. What might your mandala look like? What inspires you, drives you, and gives you a sense of vitality when you awaken each morning? Is what you do, think, and say in alignment with these energies and passions?

After letting go of the ego's fears, you'll have clarity about what will make you feel fulfilled, and you'll use your awareness to construct a realistic vision instead of a grandiose and unattainable one. We're often urged to "dream big" and to say, "the sky's the limit" and "I can do anything if I put my mind to it." This is a good first step in creating a plan, but you must also understand what's involved in manifesting that particular dream, be open to how it manifests, and be willing to work hard. This will prevent you from becoming stuck in the planning and dreaming stage.

I'll provide you with practical tools for creating and honing your vision, for researching its practicality and becoming honest with yourself about whether this is what you truly want. Using mindfulness, you can evaluate your plan from the level of the core self without becoming distracted by the distorted thoughts of the false self.

Step 3: Move Forward

In the third and final step in the art of creative transformation, you'll learn how to further hone your mandala, altering it where necessary and putting the finishing touches on this work of art—and you'll learn to recognize when it's time to sweep it away. Accepting that discomfort and suffering are a natural part of life, you'll understand that happiness ebbs and flows, and that you can't be a Zen master at all times. You'll never be able to fully eradicate the little voice in your head that harshly judges you with thoughts such as, "You're no good" or "You'll never succeed." In many ways, this voice is like an undertow in the ocean, trying to pull you out to sea and away from what you want. To be successful at surging forward, you have to learn not to be sucked into the undertow, and instead to "surf with the saboteur," that nay-saying inner voice. As a surfer, you remain balanced and continue moving forward even when, deep down, you feel unsure of yourself and long for the security of solid ground. Approaching the shore, you start to realize that you can manage the force of that uncertainty.

Very real challenges will arise when you successfully undergo a positive transformation, but you'll have learned practical ways to meet them, including how to gather and work with a *wisdom council of support* (see chapter 11). Having received the wise counsel and the creative ideas of people you respect and trust, you can use your mindfulness meditation practice to connect with your authentic self and determine the best course for you.

So open yourself up to mastering the art of creative transformation, to sweeping away the old mandala, whose sands may have already begun to blow away in the winds of change. Trust in this process, which you'll always have available to you when you need to work with the sands and the winds that are a part of life.

CHAPTER 2

How Mindfulness Helps You Transform

To enjoy good health, to bring true happiness to one's family, to bring peace to all, one must first discipline and control one's own mind.

—Buddha

An impending transition can result in your feeling lost, sad, confused, and anxious. Even if you have some idea of what direction to take, it can be very difficult to overcome inner resistance. The fear of making a mistake and experiencing suffering instead of happiness can shut down your ability to see clearly and consider all your options.

Mindfulness is the core practice in the art of creative transformation, the key to achieving open-mind consciousness. It allows you to discover your courage and let go of avoidance behaviors and resistance, tune in to your deepest inner resources, and move forward in the right direction. Cultivating mindfulness is similar to working out in a gym, but instead of building muscle, you're building what I call *mindstrength*. Mindstrength is the ability to very quickly and easily shift out of reactive mode, and become fully present in the moment, experiencing the full force of your emotions even as you recognize that they are temporary and will soon dissipate. Mindstrength gives you mastery over your thoughts and feelings, opening your eyes to whether the products of your mind are useful tools for self-discovery or merely distracting detritus. The more you cultivate mindfulness, the easier it is to stop running away from difficult feelings; to make the choice to break out of denial, stagnation, and suffering; and to act with mindful intent.

MINDSTRENGTH

Mindstrength is the ability to very quickly and easily shift out of reactive mode, and become fully present in the moment, experiencing the full force of your emotions even as you recognize that they are temporary and will soon dissipate.

THE RELATIONSHIP BETWEEN MINDFULNESS AND THE ART OF CREATIVE TRANSFORMATION

Ideas will come to you when you tune in to the enormous wealth of creativity that lies beneath the bubbling surface created by the overactive mind. Panic reactions and frantic scrambling for quick solutions to alleviate your discomfort will cease as a brilliant light slowly rises in your awareness, illuminating many paths of possibility. You may decide to make a radical change in your circumstances or adjust your situation in small but important ways. You may discover that you have the strength and wisdom to tolerate the pain of facing your current situation, and repairing and enhancing it. Alternatively, your courage may give you the impetus to move on and fashion a new mandala. Together, mindfulness and the art of creative transformation allow you to access the wisdom, insight, and deepest resources of the core self.

With mindfulness training, you first begin to watch and observe your mind in order to develop insight into how it works. As you study it, you start to see its tendency to create a sense of isolation, which can cause you to feel that you're unsupported and that solving all your problems is entirely up to you. Through this practice of moment-by-moment noting, observing, and listening to what arises in your mind, you quickly come to discover that you're not alone, that you're integrated into a vast body of billions of other beings with consciousness, all struggling to flourish and interact with effectiveness and inventiveness in an ever-changing world. The payoffs of mindfulness are feeling less anxious, more at peace with present circumstances, less lonely and fearful, and more enthusiastic about life.

At the same time, mindfulness allows you to understand that by accepting yourself exactly as you are, you'll find the courage to make internal changes that will affect your circumstances and those around you. As you ease your own suffering and discomfort, and open up to new ways of thinking and perceiving, you join in the task of transforming your relationships, your workplace, and your community.

All of this happens because you become less attuned to the unimportant chatter taking place in your mind, seeing and listening to it without becoming engaged by it, and easily discerning it as a mostly meaningless internal monologue unworthy of your attention. At the same time, as you continue your mindfulness practice and reach deeper levels of consciousness more quickly, you become more attuned to others and the quality and nature of your interactions. You'll notice the signs of trouble in your relationships early on, and have enough mindstrength to deal with them immediately, even if it's painful to confront the truth.

Mindfulness meditation, also known as *insight meditation*, means seeing the true nature of your experiences. Practiced for thousands of years, it has proved to be a remarkable tool for creative transformation. Some would say that it allows us to go beyond our personal truth and ways of perceiving, and tap into a much larger wisdom and source of innovation and inspiration, as well as our core self.

Mindfulness practice builds mindstrength, causing you to stop being reactive. You'll no longer instantaneously respond with fear to the events around you, desperate to control the powerful winds of change. I like to think of mindfulness practice as giving you the ability to surf the ever-undulating ocean of transformation rather than be engulfed by it. No matter how much time you spend practicing mindfulness or trying to prepare for life's unexpected challenges, you can't prevent the waves of pain and suffering from moving toward you. What you can do is ride atop those thought waves of the mind instead of being pulled under by them.

Mindfulness helps you leave the past behind, let go of worries about the future, and live fully in the present, where you can access your passions, talents, yearnings, and creativity, which allow you to fashion a new mandala. It does this by actually retraining the brain, laying new neural pathways that support new ways of thinking, acting, and feeling (Davidson et al. 2003).

When it comes to achieving results, mindfulness meditation is remarkably speedy and efficient. I often tell new clients that we could spend a few years together working with traditional forms of therapy to help them through a difficult transition, or speed the process along exponentially by having them establish a practice of mindfulness meditation that requires a minimum of only twenty minutes twice a day. All the suggestions I offer you in this book will be far easier to implement if you commit wholeheartedly to a mindfulness meditation practice.

A regular practice quickly leads to changes in perception. Your ability to observe and detach from your limiting thoughts and overwhelming emotions increases along with your access to your deepest level of resourcefulness. The new neural pathways wired into the mind by a mindfulness meditation practice will serve you when you're in conversation with someone you love or sitting in a meeting at work. You'll see with new eyes and feel inspired and energized as you discover exciting new possibilities.

THE EFFICIENCY AND EFFECTIVENESS OF MINDFULNESS MEDITATION

Meditators used to be told that it takes twenty or thirty years to master the skill of remaining mindful when not in meditation. We now know this isn't true. Many of my clients are resistant to trying mindfulness meditation despite my coaxing. Once they finally do it, they report that mindfulness practice very swiftly leads to more comfort with the rush of thoughts and feelings they're experiencing and to the ability to find the calm in the center of the storm. It helps them observe the unfolding of change instead of having their attention drift to the emotions and thoughts churned up by the mind. This new ability to calmly watch the process of transformation allows them the clarity of mind to find the rudder and steer the ship of change. Then, progress in therapy takes a quantum leap forward.

Knowing that regular mindfulness meditation practice has this tremendous effect on my clients, I introduce the idea very early on in treatment. In traditional psychoanalysis, it's said that in the first five years of therapy, the patient and therapist are establishing a relationship, and the real progress takes many years. Mindfulness meditation complements any treatment, allowing people to experience a sudden deepening of awareness and insight, giving them the ability to break patterns that have plagued them for years. In the transpersonal psychological approach, as articulated by Ken Wilber, genuine, deep psychological and spiritual growth are most likely to happen when a person learns on several complementary tracks at once. He refers to this learning process as an "all states, all stages, all quadrants, and all lines (AQAL) approach" (Wilber 2007, 70–72 and 151).

For many years, scientists believed that the brain's plasticity, that is, its ability to create new structures and learn, was limited after childhood. However, new research shows that we can alter the structure of the brain and reap the benefits well into adulthood. Sara Lazar, a researcher at Massachusetts General Hospital, discovered that the more one practices mindfulness meditation, the thicker the brain becomes in the mid-prefrontal cortex and in the mid-insular region of the brain. Changing your mind (or thought processes) actually causes changes in the brain (Lazar et al. 2005). Lazar found that, while people who've practiced meditation for ten or twenty years are adept at quickly achieving a state of concentration and mindful awareness, newcomers who engage in mindfulness meditation as little as four hours a week can achieve and sustain a state of mindfulness that leads to creative flow, or what I call "open-mind consciousness." She discovered that even beginning meditators in their early twenties were able to achieve advanced states of concentration and insight (what I refer to as "mindstrength") equal to that of senior meditation practitioners. Intention and attention of focus were the keys to reaching these states, not the number of hours spent on a meditation cushion (Lazar and Siegel 2007). From my own experience and work, I know that regular mindfulness practice allows us to set aside distractions and enter the transformative state of open mind.

Mindfulness practice may positively affect the amount of activity in the amygdala, the walnut-sized area in the center of the brain responsible for regulating emotions (Davidson 2000). When the amygdala is relaxed, the parasympathetic nervous system engages to counteract the anxiety response. The heart rate lowers, breathing deepens and slows, and the body stops releasing cortisol and adrenaline into the bloodstream; these stress hormones provide us with quick energy in times of danger but have damaging effects on the body in the long term if they're too prevalent. Over time, mindfulness meditation actually thickens the bilateral, prefrontal right-insular region of the brain (Lazar et al. 2005), the area responsible for optimism and a sense of well-being, spaciousness, and possibility. This area is also associated with creativity and an increased sense of curiosity, as well as the ability to be reflective and observe how your mind works.

By building new neural connections among brain cells, we rewire the brain, and with each new neural connection, the brain is actually learning. It's as if we're adding more RAM to a computer, giving it more functionality. In *The Mindful Brain*, leading neuroscientist Daniel Siegel (2007, 5), defines the mind as "a process that regulates the flow of energy and information." His early brain research showed that "where neurons fire, they can rewire" (2007, 291); that is, they create new neural pathways or structures in the brain. He postulates that one of the benefits of mindfulness meditation practice is this process of creating new neural networks for self-observation, optimism, and well-being. Through mindfulness meditation, we light up and build up the left-prefrontal cortex, associated with optimism, self-observation, and compassion, allowing ourselves to cease being dominated by the right-prefrontal cortex, which is associated with fear, depression, anxiety, and pessimism. As a result, our self-awareness and mood stability increase as our harsh judgments of others and ourselves decrease. By devoting attention, intention, and daily effort to being mindful, we learn to master the mind and open the doorway to the creativity available in open-mind consciousness.

According to research, if you're facing a change in your health status, mindfulness practice can be especially helpful, because it alleviates the stress response of the sympathetic nervous system. Jon Kabat-Zinn's mindfulness research found that when people used mindfulness meditation to help themselves heal from physical trauma, they achieved healing four times faster than those who didn't use this technique (Williams et al. 2007). Additionally, new research shows that mindfulness meditation slows the progression of HIV by stopping the decline of immunoprotective CD4 T cells, which are often destroyed by stress (Cresswell et al. 2009).

It's entirely possible that the same effects can be achieved through other practices that appear to open up new neural pathways, such as tai chi, yoga, and other forms of meditation, but thanks to researchers studying mindfulness meditation, we now know that we can actually remap the brain and affect the way it functions, as well as the way it influences the body.

HOW MINDFULNESS WORKS

Mindfulness is a process of linking awareness with attention in order to develop, expand, and enhance both. It results in more focused and heightened concentration, allowing you to note the themes unfolding in your mind and body moment by moment, rather than become immersed in the content of your thoughts, feelings, and sensations. You actually become aware that you have two selves, the self that's having the experience and the self that is witnessing it and is separate from it. This phenomenon has been called "cultivating the witness or observer," or "cultivating the witnessing mind."

First, you allow this witnessing self to emerge in your awareness. Then, instead of thinking about, analyzing, and building upon a sensation or feeling, you simply observe the thought or feeling as it arises, catalog it, and let it drift out of your awareness. Soon, after sustaining a heightened focus, the mind becomes empty of all thought as you begin the process of entering open mind and discovering your creativity and the sense of spaciousness and possibility it has to offer.

As you meditate and allow the witnessing mind to sort through sensations, beliefs, thoughts, and feelings, setting aside the ones it decides you don't need to delve into or explore, you come to understand how the mind works and choose not to assign great significance to most of what it generates. Continually observing the mind's products, identifying them, and filing them away in the "to address later" file or the proverbial "circular file" teaches you that you have power over your mind and its activities. The sad feeling, thought about the past, or heavy sensation in the heart that arises in meditation may be an indicator of thoughts, emotions, and belief systems that require attention and analysis later, when you've completed your meditation session. More likely, they're simply distracting flotsam.

The more you experience this process, the more you'll realize how temporary and unimportant many of your thoughts, feelings, sensations, and beliefs are. You'll find it easier to avoid jumping on them and riding them like a wild horse wherever they take you. They very quickly fade to become mere activity in the distance, which you can observe without any emotional response.

This dual awareness that arises when you allow the witnessing mind to emerge fosters the courage to fully experience even the most painful emotions, beliefs, and memories, and tolerate any accompanying physical sensations. Part of your awareness, the "witnessing mind," knows that you're separate from your circumstances, so you feel safer than if your awareness were completely absorbed in those thoughts and feelings. Remaining present in your suffering instead of running from it places you at the doorway to your deepest, or core, creativity. As an added benefit, mindfulness practice will help you develop greater compassion and wisdom that will serve you well in the future.

MINDFULNESS, OPEN MIND, AND CORE CREATIVITY

It's unfortunate that many people have become cut off from their natural creativity by the belief that it's something reserved for people engaged in the fine arts. We can be far too literal about what constitutes creativity. If you're driving your usual route to work and you see an accident up ahead in the road, it's creativity that allows you to quickly figure out an alternate route. If you're leading a group project and a member gets sick and can't do his part, creativity allows you to figure out whether to reassign the work, do without it, or take it on yourself. If you're in chronic pain and unable to continue at your current job, mindfulness and creativity open you up to other options. Like everyone, you have to rely on creativity in all sorts of circumstances in order to be resilient. If you deepened your creativity, what a valuable resource it would be in a time of crisis and uncertainty.

At the crossroads of change, we typically panic and become completely cut off from the source of our creative juices. The fear of not knowing what our new course should be can make us feel woefully inadequate to the challenge of reinvention and cause us to start looking outside ourselves for input and direction. While good advice and ideas are everywhere, fear makes it difficult to make good decisions based on what our core self desires, that is, the self that knows our most cherished values, desires, and passions. Instead of remaining present with the feeling and trusting that answers will arise from within—from the deepest, or core, creative self—we reach for fast, but temporary, solutions.

Your mind's usual, everyday creativity is based on thoughts and experiences you've had in the past. When you draw from this limited amount of information, you're using a restricted number of neural pathways in the brain—most likely, the ones that are well established and that you've always relied upon. If it's your habit to respond to the possibility of change with defensiveness, it's hard to lay a new neural pathway for openness without actually using a tool like mindfulness to alter your brain's wiring and structure. You're likely to do a little brainstorming and talk yourself into a modest change that has enough elements of familiarity that you won't resist it. The thoughts you haven't entertained and the experiences you've never had will remain unfamiliar. These limitations may well lead you back to the same old behaviors and ideas you've worked and reworked. Hence, accessing the resource of a deeper, or core, creativity via mindfulness meditation, generating a sense of spaciousness and receptivity, can be extremely helpful in the art of transformation. A sense of profound possibility will rush into you as if you were a lost climber wandering through a blinding snowstorm high in the mountains who suddenly discovers a clearing and is able to find her way back to the path.

The clarity provided by core creativity enables you to recognize the core of what needs to change. For example, if you're a teacher who feels dissatisfied, you might discover that it's not the school where you teach, the grade level, or the administration that has to change; it's you. You might then realize that you could direct your passion for teaching in ways you'd never considered. I have a client who teaches art in an elementary school, and she spends five minutes meditating before her students come in for a class. She says it makes her feel more receptive, passionate, and excited, so that even if she's teaching the basics of the color wheel for the hundredth time, the repetition doesn't feel deadening. Explaining that it will help them discover what images and colors they want to use in their artwork, she has her students meditate mindfully for a couple of minutes before beginning a project. Since beginning this practice, she's noticed that her students are far less likely to say, "But I don't know what to paint!" or "How am I supposed to do this?" They're more self-reliant, discovering their own ways of expressing what's inside of them instead of trying to conform to some cookie-cutter idea of what to paint and how to approach the process.

> The past should not be followed after
> and the future not desired;
> what is past is dead and gone,
> and the future is yet to come.
>
> —Majjhima Nikaya III:131

MINDFULNESS, STAGNATION, AND BREAKTHROUGHS

Because of our discomfort with change, we often passively accept stagnation, even when a situation is very dissatisfying. By blithely going along with circumstances as they are, and ignoring the evidence that we're in a deadening job or partnership, we set ourselves up for a shock when the other people in the situation decide they're ready to end it and move on.

Being mindful helps you avoid harsh wake-up calls that seem to come out of nowhere: your spouse's request for a divorce, your company's announcement of a corporate restructuring, or your body's indication that something's seriously wrong with your health. Cultivating mindfulness and developing mindstrength also allows you to find novelty in a thirty-year marriage, yet another financial meeting at work, or simply a stroll down the produce aisle in the grocery store as you plan dinner. When you infuse your life with the energy of fresh ideas and approaches, and practice mindfulness, you'll be able to see problems that arise, acknowledge them, meditate on them, and begin to address them. You can begin creatively transforming your circumstances, priming the pump for even greater breakthroughs.

Most of us have been taught that wandering through back roads with no clear goal in mind is indulgent and unproductive. We worry about the time that's passing and what's around the bend, so we try to figure out a good solution. If we can't, we simply try to cope, repressing our feelings of discomfort as best we can. We become stuck, frustrated, and afraid that we'll never find a way out.

The left brain, the seat of logic and reason, resists exploring unknown territory and opening up to unproven ideas, but these are what lead you out of stagnation and fear of change, and into the most brilliant break-throughs. Mindfulness meditation stimulates the right hemisphere of the brain and allows you to achieve open mind, where you lose your aware-ness of time, feel a sense of spaciousness, and become receptive to unseen possibilities. In this expansive state, you trust that you've connected with a source of unlimited knowledge and potential. You can listen to your inner calling and bravely follow it rather than try to quiet it out of the fear of taking a risk.

Open mind awareness carries over to your everyday life, allowing you to maintain your sense of wonder and excitement about the unknown. Just as you can experience a feeling or thought without getting completely absorbed in it, maintaining the perspective of the witness who observes, categorizes, and sets aside the feelings and thoughts that threaten to envelope you completely, you can be highly innovative yet sensible. You can cease being a flighty dreamer or an overly rigid planner, and embrace the best qualities of both.

Increased right-brain activity helps you become more creative and intuitive overall, and better able to access your unconscious mind. Some of the freshest and most original ideas are illogical on the surface, and arise from the right brain. "Thinking out of the box" means breaking out of the limitations of the logical, rational conscious mind, and bringing to your awareness the language and metaphor of visual imagery and arche-type. Dreams access that creativity, as do guided meditations and artistic or musical activity. If you want to envision something fresh and original, a life that's more fulfilling and energizing, you have to engage in contem-plation, which awakens the right brain—and that's at the core of mind-fulness meditation practice. Both the English poet William Blake—who wrote, "To see for oneself what Adam and Eve saw during those earliest moments of creation in the Garden of Eden"—and the Trappist monk Thomas Merton spoke frequently of the need to take time each day for peaceful and reflective contemplation as a direct way to enter a divine state of inner quietude and creativity.

MINDFULNESS WHILE WORKING WITH OTHERS

Allowing the witnessing mind to emerge provides you with clarity and calm in a crisis, protecting you from the temptation to panic and jump from one bad situation to another, or blame others for the crisis and avoid looking at your role in it; plus it gives you the power to change it. It allows you to tolerate the discomfort of confrontation with others and the embarrassment of discovering how you might have contributed to the problem. It also allows you to find your creativity and resourcefulness, so that you can approach the situation differently and perhaps transform it. Mindful communication is an extraordinary tool for problem solving.

One of my clients, Curt, works in a small niche industry, and he'll never be able to completely avoid interacting with his boss, even if he takes a different job within his field. Unfortunately, Curt's employer has a narcissistic personality disorder and was constantly abusive and inappropriate in his behavior toward Curt and his coworkers. Sometimes, as much as you'd like to, you can't walk away from a situation, because the price is simply too high; however, it's not healthy to remain in stagnation, hoping the problem will magically go away on its own. Mindfulness practice can create such a dramatic change in your own perceptions, thoughts, feelings, and behaviors that the situation greatly improves to the point where it has been altered almost beyond recognition.

Curt found this to be true when he began practicing mindfulness meditation and applied mindfulness and creativity to his situation. However, he also found that therapy was an important adjunct, helping him understand his boss's behavior and its origins. This insight helped Curt navigate the minefield of his boss's volatility and even experience a little more compassion for him. Curt came to recognize that the abusive behavior was not about him, which made it easier for him to remain nonreactive and, eventually, to confront his boss in a healthy, calm way and insist on some boundaries for behavior. Therapy also helped Curt understand the roots of his own psychological issues, making it easier for him to understand and accept that he had long-established patterns that weren't working for him that would take time and effort to replace.

Over time, Curt came to see that his boss was behaving toward him the same way his abusive and critical father had behaved when he was a child. Allowing the witness to emerge into his awareness enabled him to separate internally from the pain and trauma of his childhood experience, and recognize that though his boss was like his father, Curt was no longer a child and his boss wasn't a parent with complete authority over him. Curt was able to free himself from the fear and panic that had arisen whenever he'd confronted his boss or contradicted his orders. In fact, his boss came to admire Curt for standing up to him and, during business meetings, began to defer to him, showing respect and admiration.

Wherever you go, you'll find difficult and even disturbed people. Wherever you go, you always take yourself! The mindstrength and creativity cultivated through mindfulness practice and therapy or coaching will help you handle difficult people and work with them, or around them, to achieve your goals. By recognizing and accepting what's happening inside you in the present moment, you shift out of the mode of automatic reaction and remain in touch with your wisdom and ingenuity. You can be clear and calm, and, even better, find yourself coming up with ideas that seem to spring magically from somewhere deep inside you.

One of my clients, who was furious with his business partner, was marching toward her like a soldier bent on battle when suddenly his emotional experience shifted. He became aware of his partner's vulnerabilities and limitations, and observed that he didn't have to wage war against her in order to address the issue at hand. He immediately thought, "She's simply not capable in this situation, whereas I am," and knew what he would do. As he continued walking forward, he remained in a state of calm detachment as his partner, who had seen the anger flashing in his eyes, revealed, "I know, I know, you're probably mad as hell. But I just wasn't up to doing what you asked me to do." As my client described it, it was as if the self that's defined by strong emotions and limiting beliefs peeled away, allowing his core self to step into the scene. That core self immediately accessed resourcefulness and compassion. Cultivating mindfulness makes it possible for the core self to emerge in this way.

You also invite the core self to come forth into your consciousness when you disengage from a conflict by physically leaving the situation, shifting your emotions, or redirecting the conversation to a more productive dialogue. Reactivity lessens, and you're able to remain present with the discomfort and acknowledge what's going on underneath the surface. You may even be able to shift gears through humor or an expression of compassion toward the other person, immediately taking the negative charge out of the interaction. When you create a space for dialogue and begin the process of letting go of your suffering, you invite others to join you. They feel encouraged to tolerate the discomfort of difficult thoughts and feelings, discuss them with you, and come to creative resolutions.

The ability to engage in constructive conflict is an absolutely invaluable skill for creative transformation—and it's one that mindfulness helps you develop. Your newfound mindstrength will give you the courage to acknowledge your own role in any situation and your power to change the way you think, act, or feel, and to stop seeing yourself as a passive sufferer.

You may not be able to change others, but you can make a choice to speak honestly, without fear or intimidation, and invite them to engage in a healthier interaction in order to salvage and enhance your relationship. Then again, you can also recognize when you feel you must leave a situation, and do it without second-guessing whether it's the right decision or experiencing regrets afterward. Mindfulness gives you the clarity to set good boundaries and the courage to enforce them. However choppy the waters, you can remain poised atop the surfboard and move forward without being pulled under. In the next chapter, you'll learn the basics of establishing a mindfulness meditation practice so that you can take out that surfboard and start riding the waves.

CHAPTER 3

The Basics of
Mindfulness Meditation

The way of the Buddha is to know yourself;
To know yourself is to forget yourself;
To forget yourself is to be awakened by all things.

—Dogen

Mindfulness meditation practice is a commitment that many resist, but it requires far less time and effort than most people realize. For best results, practice mindfulness meditation for twenty to thirty minutes twice a day in a quiet room with a closed door and no distractions. If you travel a lot, you can do it on a train, plane, or bus, or even in a waiting room or traffic jam. The more you practice, the easier it will be to center yourself amid the distractions. You'll hear the phone ring, the children playing downstairs, or people walking in the hallway and talking just outside your office, and it won't bother you. You'll observe the sound, note it, and categorize it as background noise that can be ignored.

One of the concerns about meditating that my clients often have is the fear that if they quiet down, a great idea will come to them and they'll have no way of capturing it before it leaves their consciousness. I recommend having a pen and pad of paper nearby, in case you feel the urge to write down something that seems important, whether it's a creative idea or the sudden awareness that you've left an important task off your agenda. The idea is to simply record that creative idea or important task but not give it attention until you're finished meditating. If you complete your meditation session, you'll actually have more energy and creativity to work, and you'll be able to set aside any anxiety or frustration and explore your options. I've found that occasionally breaking the classic rule of never stopping the meditation during a session, and choosing instead to jot down important thoughts, can allow you to focus better on the meditation instead of continually wrestling with a persistent thought. Most of the time, however, simply noting the thoughts or images and coming back to them later, after you come out of the meditative state, is the best course.

Many of my clients choose to start the day with a meditation session and do another before work, midday (perhaps on a lunch break), before dinner, or just before going to bed. The time of day isn't important; the regular practice is. It's better to start by doing ten minutes once a day than to aim for the eventual goal of two twenty-minute sessions per day and fall short by meditating for twenty minutes one day and not again until a few days later, when you remember your promise to yourself. Use a timer to ensure that you meditate for as long as you'd planned. Aim for meditating at the same time in the same quiet and serene place, such as sitting down in your office chair for the first time in the morning or sitting in your car as you prepare to drive home from the gym after your daily workout. Again, choose a time when distractions will be minimal.

Whenever you know that your schedule will be altered due to travel, having houseguests, and so on, plan for how you'll work in your meditation. I travel a lot, and I always inform the people sponsoring my workshop that I'll need to block out forty-five minutes in the early morning before my teaching day begins and forty-five minutes in the late afternoon in order to meditate.

If you anticipate a stressful situation in which it will be challenging for you to remain nonreactive or in which you'll need to access your creativity more than usual because you're dealing with a perplexing problem, try to schedule a mindfulness meditation immediately beforehand. I've had clients meditate before attending a late-afternoon meeting in order to refresh themselves creatively, and before a phone conversation with an ex-spouse, and they've reported that just five minutes spent in mindfulness practice makes a dramatic difference in their ability to remain calm, focused, and nonreactive.

HOW TO PERFORM MINDFULNESS MEDITATION

Here are the four steps of mindfulness meditation:

STEP 1: GET INTO A COMFORTABLE POSTURE. Sit cross-legged on a meditation cushion or with your legs extended straight out, with your back against a wall for support, or sit in a chair with a firm back, keeping your feet on the floor and your spine straight, and tucking in your chin slightly to keep your vertebrae aligned properly. If you have any back, pelvic, or neck pain, back support is essential. In fact, you may want to lie on the floor, or on a couch or bed, with your head propped up at a forty-five-degree angle. Alternatively, sit in an ergonomic office chair with lumbar support.

If you're sitting up, close your eyes, but if you're lying down, keep your eyes half open to prevent yourself from falling asleep.

STEP 2: FOCUS YOUR EYES. With your eyes closed, focus them on one spot. You may wish to focus them toward the tip of your nose or on your "third eye" (the chakra, or energy point, identified in yogic and meditative systems), the area in the middle of the forehead. Allow your eyeballs to roll upward. Alternatively, look straight ahead at the insides of your eyelids. Whichever eye position you choose, make certain it feels comfortable and that your eye muscles are relaxed. You can also focus on the muscles at the back of your eyes, relaxing them.

If you have heightened anxiety or fears, or are dealing with a trauma, you may want to open your eyes halfway or even fully, looking straight ahead at a spot on the wall or out the window at a stationary object, in order to ease those feelings. For example, try sitting about three feet from the wall, and with your back straight, slightly tilt your head downward and find the spot where the wall and floor meet. With your eyes slightly open and relaxed, gaze steadily at this point. You may also wish to close your eyes and imagine being in a place where you always felt relaxed, safe, and secure, such as when you were a child sitting on your grandmother's lap or on the swing in your backyard. You might even imagine such a spot if you can't remember one. This will immediately assist you in decreasing your anxiety and any inner fear about entering into a meditative state.

STEP 3: PAY ATTENTION TO YOUR BREATHING. With your eyes closed, fixating them on one spot, breathe in with awareness of your lungs and your diaphragm. As you inhale, say to yourself, "In." Exhale from your lungs and then your abdomen, saying to yourself, "Out." Do this each time you breathe. You can also use the words "rising" and "falling away," or "comfort" and "letting go," or "surrender" and "release."

STEP 4: PLACE YOUR HANDS IN A RELAXING AND ENER-GIZING MUDRA (HAND POSITION). In Buddhism, the *mudra*, or position of the hands, in meditation is important, because it affects the flow of energy throughout the body. There are three traditional mudras: (1) The first is to touch the thumb and first finger to each other, and then hold your palms up, with your other fingers relaxed and straight, and rest the backs of your hands on your thighs. (2) The second, which is more common in Zen Buddhism, is similar: you bring your gently cupped hands together at your abdomen, thumbs facing away from you and palms up, with the fingernails of your first three fingers touching. (3) The third, also a Zen mudra, is to hold your right hand in your lap or at your navel, with the palm turned upward, thumb facing away from you, and other fingers straight; then place your left hand on top of the right hand, also palm up with the thumb facing away from you so that your two thumbs form a triangle with your left index finger.

STEP 5: BE AWARE. As you breathe in and out, mentally note the thoughts, feelings, sounds, tastes, smells, and physical sensations (such as itching, temperature, pain or discomfort, or feelings of heaviness and lightness) that you experience. Don't try to analyze any of what you're noting. Simply be present, open, alert, and watchful as you allow the witnessing mind to emerge. Observe the quality of the sensation if it has one, and categorize it: "heaviness in shoulders," "bitter taste," "lawn mower outside," "painful thought about son," "thought about that call I should make," and so on.

Don't explore this thought or feeling unless it occurs more than twice, in which case, ask yourself, "Is this something I can come back to later, after I've meditated?" If the answer is yes, let go of the thought as you exhale, but do come back to it later and write about it in your mindfulness journal (which I introduce later in this chapter), contemplate it, or talk to a friend or counselor about it. If you determine that what keeps coming up for you should be addressed right away, allow yourself to be present with that sensation, feeling, or repetitive thought. At the same time, allow the witness aspect of your consciousness to observe yourself without judgment as the feeling, thought, or sensation fades away or lessens in intensity.

STEP 6: SLOWLY COME BACK INTO ORDINARY CONSCIOUSNESS. Take three long, slow, deep breaths, breathing in through your nose and out through your mouth. Rub the palms of your hands together to generate heat, and place the palms over your eyes and face. Open your eyes and slowly lift your hands away from your face as you return to awareness. Inhale deeply and stretch your arms up over your head, with your hands interlocked. Bend slowly to the right and then to the left. Do this several times, and then bend forward toward your feet. Reflect on whether anything of importance revealed itself to you that you wish to write about in your mindfulness journal, think about, or attend to.

THE MINDFULNESS JOURNAL

I suggest you create and work with a mindfulness journal, a blank book that you can use to record your sensations, observations, thoughts, feelings, emotions, images, creative ideas, and messages of wisdom from your mind and body as you become mindful of them. These may come to you as you perform the exercises in this book, along with insights and images that you would like to explore later. When you write, be mindful of simply noting what you've experienced and why you might have experienced it.

You may also want to arrange your schedule so that you can commit to sitting quietly and writing in your mindfulness journal. It's best to do this in a peaceful, restful place, perhaps a room in which you're surrounded by books and pictures that inspire you and evoke qualities such as wisdom and joy. You may also want to sit on a meditation chair or cushion with meditative music playing, wrap yourself in a meditation shawl or blanket, and light a candle or incense. Be certain to set aside a time when you won't be disturbed.

CATEGORIZING WHAT THE MIND CHURNS UP

Our minds create a mix of emotions, thoughts, and sensations, all of which influence each other. The thought, "My boss is so insensitive; I can't believe he was so abrupt with me today," might not surface in your mind until you sit and begin meditating, and might appear not as a fully formed thought but as a headache or an overall sense of vulnerability and defensiveness. In meditation, it's important not to go wherever those sensations and feelings take you but to simply sit with them, allowing them to reveal themselves. Afterward, as you write in your journal about your experience, work with a therapist, or ponder where that feeling or sensation came from, you might discover that it has deeper roots. Recognizing that your experience bears a powerful emotional resemblance to a past experience can be a helpful and freeing insight, but in the end, the story of its origin is just a story that can distract you from healing. If you come to realize that your defensiveness around your gruff boss reminds you of the way you reacted to your highly critical father, the value in that insight is acknowledging how deeply your mind has been programmed to respond to criticism or abruptness with fear and defensiveness. It's easier to be patient with yourself when you recognize that your mind has actually created an elaborate neural network to support this reaction, because clearly, it will take time, patience, and repetition to change that instantaneous response.

The danger in giving too much weight to such a revelation is that you can begin reinforcing that reality. You reinforce your habitual thinking and feeling patterns when you subscribe to a narrative of suffering such as, "I can't help being the way I am. My defensiveness goes way back to my childhood." I call this the "big story." It has the potential to shut you off from the art of creative transformation. Once you've identified the big story, categorize it as "old stuff" and set it aside whenever it comes up. The major healing work most people need to do is to transform and move beyond the story of their relationship with their parents. The other common big stories I often encounter are "I need more money in order to be happy and secure" and "No one gives me credit for all I do." There's no benefit in bringing back all of the details of your big story, retelling it to yourself over and over again. It was what it was, and now that you're aware of it, you can let go of it and replace it with a new, more positive and creative story that will make you feel freed from your past.

It's also important to let go of the "new stuff": each "small story," or rationalization for why your present life is the way it is. The small stories are worth examining to discover what lessons they hold, but if you hang on to them, repeating them to yourself, they become "old stuff" and part of the big story as well. Your friend may have communication problems that make it difficult for you to be nonreactive and remain the observer when he starts speaking flippantly to you. It's helpful to explore what you can do to affect your friend's communication problems, but you may soon realize that he isn't willing to be mindful of his behavior and consider changing it. In that case, your own ability to remain mindful, a witness to the drama unfolding before you, will give you the clarity and courage to either accept the situation as it is (without being drawn into an emotional response) or change the situation by ending the friendship.

As long as you remain in these stories, you create suffering for yourself. To change your life, you have to see the story for what it is: a way of framing events that doesn't contribute to your happiness and holds you back from positive change. Holding on to your story, big or small, giving it life in retelling and embellishing it endlessly, will cause you pain. The point isn't whether or not you're justified in telling that particular story, or its veracity, but whether you're suffering because of it.

When you set aside your thoughts and feelings, you're not engaging in avoidance behavior. Mindfulness training is not about denial; it's about the acceptance of what's emerging from inside you moment by moment and dealing with it appropriately. It takes practice to develop the acceptance that the content of most of the thoughts your mind creates isn't very important. The more you meditate, the more it will feel as if you're simply sorting the laundry as you observe what your mind generates. You may be surprised by just how many "socks" you own. Old thoughts and feelings about unworthiness may come up in many different forms, but none of them matters if you choose not to assign them significance. Over time, your distracting feelings, thoughts, and sensations will dissipate, and you'll find that you're doing less sorting as you sit in mindfulness.

Four Myths About Mindfulness Meditation That Cause Resistance

The majority of my clients resist mindfulness meditation at first, although the time commitment is small and the payoff is enormous. One of my clients insisted that it wasn't necessary and that she didn't have enough time in her day to devote to a regular practice. She said that taking twenty minutes twice a day was a "virtual impossibility," but when she went through the loss of a parent, she had such trouble coping that she couldn't even drag herself out of bed. After she'd called in sick to work ten days straight, she called me to ask what she could do, because she knew she had to get back to the office. I told her to mindfully meditate while in bed. Terrified and bewildered, my client took this advice and, in a few days, found that she could face going to work again. After that, she called me up several times to say that she was in an overwhelming state of grief or so distracted that she couldn't focus during crucial meetings, and my advice was always the same: "Shut the door and tell your assistant to hold all calls and visitors. Schedule these meditation sessions as if they were a meeting with your most important client." Slowly, her grief lessened.

Typically, those who resist meditation are buying in to one of four common myths that must be discarded because they create resistance to regular mindfulness meditation practice.

Myth 1: "Practicing mindfulness meditation will conflict with my religious beliefs." The practice of mindfulness meditation for cultivating awareness is a part of good mental hygiene. Just as you turn the lights out before retiring for the night so that you're prepared to shift into another state of consciousness, you can use mindfulness meditation to take you from one state into another. This form of meditation turns down the volume of the chatter in your mind and allows you to tune in to deeper wisdom and insight.

As a method for developing awareness, mindfulness practice is free of religious and spiritual dogma. In fact, if you believe in turning to God for guidance, you can use mindfulness meditation to set aside distractions and listen to the divine wisdom that can be found only when you set aside the endless chain of thoughts your own mind creates. When you become receptive, you'll find that you're capable of cultivating silence and a deep, abiding sense of wisdom. Christian author and monk Thomas Merton, author of *The Asian Journal of Thomas Merton* (1968), had a deep appreciation for the overlap between Christian contemplative meditation and Buddhist mindfulness meditation.

Mindfulness meditation is a core practice that's referred to as *Shamatha training* in Buddhist meditation systems and Zen Buddhist practice. *Zen* actually means discovering and finding one's own truth (*Theraveda* means "the ancient teachings"), and mindfulness meditation is focused on gaining experiential knowledge. Buddhist author Stephen Batchelor has pointed out that Zen is a form of Buddhism that can include beliefs, or not (Batchelor 1997). Some would say that when we practice mindfulness meditation, we first enter deeply into the moment, and then become open to going beyond our personal truth and tapping into a much larger wisdom and source of creativity, or the truth of the divine. Others would say that we're tapping into the collective unconscious of all humanity. Either interpretation is valid. Mindfulness practice is a pathway to discovery that any of us can use, regardless of our religious or spiritual beliefs.

MYTH 2: "I'M TOO RESTLESS AND BUSY TO LEARN TO BE QUIET AND PRACTICE ANY FORM OF MEDITATION."

Just twenty minutes on a meditation cushion twice each day will cause you to need less sleep, be more productive and less distracted, and make the most of your time during the day. Note that if you're very busy, your unmindful activity may be inefficient. Many of us sit down to work at a computer and soon find that instead of simply looking up one fact on the Internet, as we'd intended, we've just spent twenty minutes watching online videos or reading a blog. If it's not a task that takes us off course, it's a distracting interaction with others. A lengthy conversation about what might happen or what should've happened in the past may be less productive than we'd like to think. We turn the same thoughts over in our minds again and again, and even work ourselves into a state of agitation—and then we find someone else to "vent" to, wasting more time.

Meditation offers two important benefits that help reduce restlessness. One is heightened concentration, allowing you to be more productive.

Another is physiological changes, namely, a decrease in skin temperature and increase in oxygenation of the brain, a decrease in lactic acid (which causes fatigue) and cortisol (a stress hormone), and a decreased need for sleep (Maupin 1990). With less fatigue and stress, you become less distracted and more efficient in using and managing your time. Ray Kroc, who took over McDonald's in its early days and built it into a business of outstanding success, once reported that he'd spontaneously fall into states of meditative reverie during the day and thus didn't need a lot of sleep (Bennis 1984). Even if you can only devote five minutes a day to mindful meditation because you're so busy, doing it while waiting in line at the bank or sitting in traffic, or waiting on hold for computer technical support, you can receive these benefits.

Restless, obsessive thinking is often mistaken for positive creative energy. Indeed, when you're obsessing, the mind is creating *something*, but on closer inspection, it's generating the same unproductive old beliefs and ideas, just in a different form. Nothing is learned or gained. When you rest your mind and let go of the constantly buzzing thoughts that pull you into the cloud of obsession, you can begin to see more clearly. You start to recognize how limited your perceptions have been and start making better decisions about how to move forward.

If you're restless or usually find it difficult to focus, you may want to practice mindfulness meditation after physical activity to calm the agitated mind and foster concentration. Yoga, in particular, can be very helpful for taking you out of your thoughts and focusing your awareness on your body. Gardening, or walking or biking in the woods or along the beach puts you in touch with the slower rhythms of nature and helps the witness or observer to rise to the surface of your awareness. Although these activities have benefits on their own, if you additionally establish a regular mindfulness meditation practice, you'll find it even easier to access your deepest wisdom and core creativity. In mindfulness meditation, there's very little sensory stimulation to pull your thoughts in one direction or another. In every sitting, thoughts, feelings, sounds, and sensations will arise, but there's no need to assign importance to any of them. Over time, you'll find it easier to move from sorting through what the mind generates moment by moment to adeptly clearing your thoughts and becoming calm and still.

When you first begin to meditate, you're likely to experience many mental distractions. Rather than judge yourself as a bad meditator; distract yourself further by obsessing over your distractibility; or create thoughts such as "Maybe I should stop meditating and make that phone call, just in case I forget," simply observe any disruptive thoughts, feelings, or sensations and set them aside. You'll never have complete freedom from distractions while meditating, but with practice, it'll be easier to quickly turn down the volume on them. Just as you can gradually build your muscles by going to the gym and developing the ability to lift weights without feeling, "I can't do this," or quickly becoming fatigued, you can build your focusing abilities through regular practice of mindfulness meditation. As your concentration abilities increase, so will your mind-strength. Quickly, you'll discover that you can simply rest and relax into the moment, enjoying the sense of spaciousness and abundance.

MYTH 3: "IF I PRACTICE MINDFULNESS, IT WILL PUT OUT THE FIRE OF MY AMBITION AND CREATIVITY." Some

of my extremely talented and creative clients are bipolar or suffer from other severe mood disorders. They're convinced that their highly active and creative minds are generating a fast-moving river of excellent ideas. One client brought me a couple of notebooks filled with stream-of-consciousness writing she was certain would, with a little editing, yield a brilliant novel. To her, the notebooks proved that a highly active mind is a far superior creative tool to a mind quieted by mindfulness meditation. But as we looked more closely at her writing, she began to see that her daylong session had actually produced little of value. It wasn't until she began mindfully meditating that her writing became more deeply creative and focused. There was less of it, because she would only write for a few hours at a time, but it was of higher quality.

Mindfulness practice seems to ground restless people, transforming their energy from a chaotic, even manic, discharge to a more focused and heightened exuberance that then can be channeled into productivity. It's important to become adept at slowing down the rush of mind flow and learn to better distinguish between core creative flow and mere mental distraction.

Some of my clients in the film, television, and music industries have resisted mindfulness meditation for five or six years and suffered through torturous manic, depressive, and anxious states, insisting they need these moods to be creative or to keep their "edge." When they finally agreed to establish a practice, they discovered that their creativity didn't disappear after all, and that they didn't need to feel competitive and aggressive in order to do their best work. Letting go of that belief, opening up to their core creativity, and trusting that there's no shortage of ideas relieved them of anxiety and a sense that they had to work nonstop lest their creative juices dry up. In each case, they also benefited from participating in mindfulness-based, mind-body therapeutic counseling, and most benefited from taking an antidepressant medication, such as Zoloft, Prozac, or Lexapro, as well.

I've found that for many bipolar people, it's not the meditation they resist so much as the idea of meditation as a healing antidote for their condition when it creates exuberant episodes. Their resistance ebbs after I explain that mindfulness practice will actually enhance their creativity. If you're uncomfortable with the thought of slowing down your mental output because you think you'll lose something valuable, keep in mind that this is not the goal of mindfulness practice. You may want to speak to your prescribing professional about reducing the dosage levels of the medication you're on after you've established a mindfulness practice and begun therapy. This approach will allow you to access some of the vitality and passion you associate with mania.

MYTH 4: "IF I PRACTICE MINDFULNESS, WHAT I'LL DISCOVER WILL BE SO UPSETTING THAT I'LL BECOME PARALYZED WITH FEAR." The fear of what will arise from the subconscious isn't entirely irrational, but the chances of experiencing intense discomfort while mindfully meditating are slim. An afflictive mind state, in which you're gripped by anxiety or feelings of sadness, anger, or unworthiness, isn't pleasant, but allowing those emotions to surface and feeling them fully lets you begin the process of working through them. Emotions that remain buried have no chance of dissipating, and will remain as an underlying toxin that affects the functioning of the mind and body. A skilled psychologist or mindfulness meditation teacher can be enormously helpful in guiding you through these emotions and modulating their intensity.

If you've been avoiding painful feelings and thoughts for a long time, you may not be able to handle more than a five-minute-long session of mindfulness meditation, and you may need someone with you to support you in your process of uncovering this pain. Most Western mindfulness meditation teachers who teach at major centers in America, regardless of how many years' experience they have, are in or have been in counseling or psychotherapy to work on their personal issues.

What does commonly emerge from meditation is physical pain. I had one client who, shortly after beginning her practice, experienced intense pain in her head whenever she sat down to meditate. After several weeks of attempting to sit in meditation and remain present with the pain instead of ending her session in order to avoid it, she found that this pain was beginning to transform into a deep feeling of anger. I encouraged her to experience the anger and let it go. In therapy, we explored the big story as well as her small stories, so she was able to recognize that the anger that was coming up had nothing to teach her because she already knew its source. Soon, the anger subsided as well, and her meditation sessions were uninterrupted by such intense feelings and sensations.

Occasionally, however, memories of the past are so horrific that instead of tranquility and calmness, mindfulness meditation can bring up feelings that are deeply upsetting. Traditionally, since this practice was rooted in ancient Asian culture, meditation teachers were usually unfamiliar with psychodynamic disorders such as those caused by trauma and abuse, and didn't give great weight to the complexity of pain and suffering associated with interpersonal relationships. Unfortunately, students who reported that frightening or extremely painful feelings and memories were coming up for them were told, "You're not trying hard enough. You need to sit longer with this pain, and it will pass." Consequently, many meditators were left with a dismal sense of failure. As Buddhist psychiatrist Mark Epstein wrote in the article, "Awakening with Prozac," in the magazine *Tricycle* (1993), meditators with a high amount of anxiety and a greater than average propensity for depression often find that the meditative experience significantly improves when they use antidepressant medication. Due to trauma or genetics, some people's brains are wired in such a way that no matter how much meditation they do, or what type of meditation they engage in, they simply can't get past their hindrances and experience the creative bliss in open mind. Their fear, anxiety, or sadness is so highly magnified that they need biochemical help to shift out of unwholesome states of mind.

So, while meditation can bring up difficult feelings, emotions, and thoughts, it's always better to uncover them and deal with their intensity rather than deny them out of fear of the discomfort they'll cause.

Some people avoid meditation because their religious beliefs cause them to fear opening the door to the subconscious; they see it as a portal to dark energies. When we access the right brain, negative thoughts, feelings, and beliefs that had been hidden in the unconscious can come tumbling through. Some people believe that because of the negative quality of such thoughts and feelings, they're the products of some external, sinister force that may even be powerful enough to take over the mind. In reality, negative beliefs and feelings are far more destructive when they remain hidden from our awareness. Bringing them into the light and consciously choosing to dismiss their significance is the only way to prevent them from unduly influencing us.

By cultivating mindfulness, you allow yourself to hear even the subtlest messages from the unconscious. You can be awakened with a gentle nudge instead of a splash of icy water. The process of necessary and inevitable transformation can begin without your being shaken out of your complacency and denial by unwanted changes imposed upon you. Embracing your circumstances despite the pain, you can craft a fulfilling life that's infused with passion and originality, driven by a sense of purpose, and in sync with your values and priorities. You can then eliminate any hidden resistance.

PART II

Let Go: Detaching from What's Holding You Back

CHAPTER 4

Understanding the Payoffs of Resistance

Creation means finding the new world
in that first fierce step,
with no thought of return.

—David Whyte, "Statue of Buddha"

Why are some people able to embrace the process of transformation so easily that they evolve seemingly without effort, while others get stuck, afraid to make a move, hoping in vain that the change they desire will come about magically and painlessly? Some are just born with a natural resilience and thirst for adventure that causes them to be comfortable with and even seek change. Others have mastered the art of creative transformation. If they feel any internal resistance, they're able to acknowledge it, work through it, and trust that this process will allow them to reinvent themselves and return to a feeling of joy and contentment. They've learned that openness and awareness are at the heart of the process, and that they must let go of the room limitations of the mind and its endless need to be in control of all changes. They recognize that the mind's role is to deconstruct the hidden beliefs creating resistance, to identify and let go of the emotions that solidify roadblocks, and to follow the heart's directives.

Traditionally, we've been told that to achieve happiness, we should use our minds to figure out what would make us happy and then work hard to achieve our goal. The problem is that even the sharpest, most clever mind is limited in its ability to create opportunities and see possibilities. Without guidance from the heart, we're merely playing notes on a piano, not composing a melody. To move out of suffering and back into contentment and joy, we must listen to the music that calls to us from our hearts and go where it takes us.

The greatest melody will never be heard if we don't touch our fingers to the keys of the piano to play it or open our mouths to sing it. Similarly, no vision, no matter how heartfelt, can manifest through mere will or intention. We need to follow through with action.

Most people desire change, and even radical change, because their lives are out of sync with their most heartfelt longings. Yet, when they're faced with overwhelming evidence that it's time to move on, to let go of what was and enter into their deepest, or core, creativity, where all sorts of overlooked possibilities will begin to reveal themselves to them, they freeze in fear. Resistance takes over.

If your resistance is stronger than your desire for a better situation, you must find your courage and delve deeply into your psyche. There, you can discover this resistance, break it apart, and access the fuel of your passion. This passion will pull you out of your routine and resistance, and into the creative process, opening your eyes to infinite possibilities. Freed from the burden of creating avoidance behaviors and repressing your anxiety and fears about change, you'll be invigorated.

To access your power to transform, you must start by exploring and dissolving your deeply rooted resistance to change.

THE PAYOFFS OF RESISTANCE TO CHANGE

Resistance to change is driven by fear. If you take a close look at the roots of that fear and address them, your resistance is likely to melt away, because you'll see that change doesn't have to be unpleasant or lead to a worse situation. You'll recognize the possibility of a positive transformation and a positive outcome.

However, while fear lies at the heart of resistance, so does a hidden payoff. All change involves loss. Holding on to what you have has benefits that your unconscious mind is aware of and hopes to maintain. The unconscious mind thinks emotionally, not rationally. So, while you may decide that, indeed, it's time to move forward and try something new, the unconscious mind steps on the brakes. It's unwilling to let go of the hidden payoffs of resistance, which, though quite real, are, upon examination, outweighed by the potential for a far more rewarding, fulfilling future situation.

Make no mistake: the emotion-driven unconscious benefits from these payoffs, because it's fearful and values security above all else. Resistance can slow down the transformation process, helping you to hold on to what you had just a little while longer. However, change and loss are inevitable. The payoffs of resistance are always short-lived.

Hidden payoffs and sources of resistance can sabotage any conscious plan for transformation that you have, so it's important to recognize them and deconstruct them. Then you can be released from the grip of fear.

PAYOFF 1: BY RESISTING CHANGE, WE CAN AVOID THE UNKNOWN. What's familiar may not be terribly comfortable, but sometimes it seems that the devil we know is better than the devil we don't know. We fear that venturing into the unknown will cause us to discover painful secrets about the world and ourselves that have been hidden from us. We take an attitude similar to that of Don Corleone in the film *The Godfather*: "This is my family and the business we have chosen." We don't think about whether change will allow us to feel more fulfilled.

In 1968, the Beatles released an album with a stark, all-white cover embossed with the words "The Beatles," a blank slate that provided no clue to what type of music was inside. The band wanted people to approach the Beatles anew, with no preconceived notions. At times of transition, all of us need to strip ourselves of the old identity so that we can explore who we are beyond our limited perceptions of ourselves, and beyond what others have told us about who we are and what we can do. It can be a scary proposition, but it's an important undertaking for anyone hoping to discover a wider range of opportunities.

Most of the time, we approach a new project, job, or relationship by clinging to what has worked for us in the past and drawing upon our limited ideas about what will work for us in the future. We remember the mistakes we made with "the ex," and are afraid of repeating them, but we don't take the time to imagine how we might act differently this time. We go back to the old formula and tinker with it superficially rather than immerse ourselves in open mind, letting go of our thoughts, facing that white album cover and blank recording tape, and allowing ideas to arise from the creative soup. Imagine that it's 1968, and the Beatles decide to trim their hair just a bit, hire a new photographer for the album-cover shot of the group, and add one new and daring composition to the usual set of pop songs about love—and cross their fingers that everyone will love the new record. Too often, we go with what worked in the past rather than peer into the unknown, where a far more interesting work of art may lie.

One of the ways we prevent ourselves from entering the creative process is by letting ourselves slip into unconscious patterns of avoidance. For example, one of my clients, Jared, a website designer, told me he truly wanted to create a plan for attracting more lucrative jobs and clients who offered steady work, but he could never seem to find the time.

I asked Jared to tell me everything he had done that morning, from the moment he woke up to the moment he came into my office. He said that he'd started his day by jumping into the shower and thinking about getting all of his distractions out of the way, and mentally going over his to-do list. He had breakfast and made a few phone calls, then sat down at his computer and read his favorite websites and blogs for two hours while answering text messages from friends. Then he realized that it was just about time to set off for my office. Jared said he'd thought about meditating before our session but felt that it was more important to check his e-mail again, and before he knew it, it was time to go.

"You did a lot this morning," I said. "Let's spend a moment and simply breathe."

For several minutes, we meditated together, and then he broke the silence: "A lot of what I was doing really wasn't a priority."

I said nothing.

"I know what you're going to say," Jared said, "of all the 'chores' I should have done this morning, I should have stopped to meditate, because if I had, I might've realized that time was slipping away from me."

"Yes, you could've done that," I said. "If you had, what might you have noticed?"

After a long pause, he said, "That I'm afraid. I'm not sure I can command top-dollar clients or manage a lot of clients. And I'm shy. I hate calling people cold or sending blind e-mails soliciting work. I wait for work to come to me, and I hold on to my clients, even the ones who waste a lot of my time, because I'm afraid I won't find better ones."

Like many of us, Jared was a little fearful of success. What would happen if he stepped out of his comfort zone and took some risks? If he were to become a busy and well-paid website designer and entrepreneur, who would he be? How would people perceive him? Would his less successful friends abandon him? Would he become more like his father, a successful entrepreneur who was a challenging person and distant parent, preoccupied with his work?

And would Jared enjoy designing websites full time, or would he find it difficult, frustrating, or isolating? Would he be able to compete with other website designers? Not knowing the answers, he was subconsciously giving in to fear.

Once you've become mindful and recognized that you've slipped into avoidance behavior, you can immediately shift out of this fear with the simple thought, "I want to go forward into my future life as a _____ [website designer, entrepreneur, student, or whatever it is that you want to do]." You can look at the subconscious thoughts and fears that are holding you back, stop identifying with them, and let them float out of your awareness like clouds drifting across the sky. If they return, you can decide not to become attached to them and follow them wherever they take you. Instead, you can simply become curious and ponder their origin. In exploring your fears and thoughts, you might have an insight that would help you to move forward with greater self-awareness, and away from the limitations you set for yourself that box you in.

Jared realized that he took comfort in knowing who he was and what his limitations were. He was letting the old belief stand in his way: "I'm a creative website designer who can't make a lot of money, because I'm the type who needs to deal with just a few, familiar clients and not feel pressured to meet a lot of demands." He wasn't taking action to satisfy his longing to have more professional successes and achieve his other goals, such as having the money to travel and buy a condominium. He needed to be aware of this self-sabotaging belief and actively choose to let go of it so that he could move into the unknown future in which he was a busy, well-paid entrepreneur with several well-paying clients, whatever that experience turned out to be like. He needed to recognize his power to decide how many clients he would take on, and to realize that he was a different person from his father and could set up his own business in a way that worked for him. In time, he discovered that he was quite capable of handling several clients and negotiating good deals for himself, without feeling that he had turned into a cold workaholic.

Instead of looking at the journey into the unknown as an exciting adventure, we typically perceive it as a dark forest full of dangerous creatures waiting to pounce on us. As Jared procrastinated about growing his business, his subconscious mind was secretly thinking about all of those imaginary predators.

This fear of the unknown is rooted in childhood. A toddler is both excited and fearful of her first small steps away from her mother as she ventures forth. In fact, it's a natural part of development for a baby to develop separation anxiety that peaks around twelve months of age, when she begins to walk and becomes aware that in doing so, she can walk away from her mother—and her mother can walk away from her. The process of separation and individuation can cause both a powerful feeling of strength and awareness of the self as separate from others, as well as the terrifying feeling of distance or separateness from the mother and a sense of abandonment. In an instant, the child stops in her tracks, turns back toward the known, and reaches for the familiar. If her parents can let go of their own fears of being abandoned by the child, they can encourage her to try again, reminding her that they'll be there, a few steps behind her, when she's ready to return.

In our adulthood, we continue to have separation anxiety but stifle our innate potential for change in more subtle ways: We get a job, hold on to it, grow with it, and then stay with it even when it's no longer working for us. We remain in a relationship even if we, as well as our partner, are deeply unhappy, hoping that the spark will magically return without our having to make any changes. We surround ourselves with people of the same social class and background so we can avoid the discomfort of questioning our choices and values, or exposing ourselves to the unfamiliar. We're afraid to break out and think differently. Again and again, we decide to stick with what we know rather than reach, even though we claim to desire change. Real change requires that we let go of our limited ideas and begin to imagine what has yet to be imagined, whether it's a new job, a new lifestyle, a new attitude, or a new way of interacting with the people in our lives. We must replace our fear and resistance with trust and faith.

Mindfulness can help us move forward through the dark jungle and thick fog of the unknown despite our fear, empowering us to take productive action. Mindfulness creates a container for the mind and its relentlessly anxious thoughts. Rather than having them swirl around us and whip themselves up into a storm of fear that paralyzes us, we can observe them in a detached way and make a conscious decision to redirect the mind where we want it to go.

PAYOFF 2: WE CAN AVOID BEING JUDGED AS "STRANGE."

Parents who are solid in their own sense of self possess the capacity to instill in a child the belief that being different, using the imagination, and taking risks that result in change is something to be valued, admired, and rewarded. They allow their child's creative energies to stream forth, even as they provide guidance that serves as a cauldron, containing the child's uniqueness and letting it percolate and simmer until it becomes a positive force instead of a destructive one.

When parents are frightened by their child's differentness, labeling it as "strange," they'll usually try to stifle his creativity. The child, sensing their disapproval and fearing abandonment, shuts down the creative flow or tries not to express his creativity and then either tries to conform to his parents' expectations or acts out, claiming not to care what anyone thinks of him. As a boy, painter and sculptor Salvador Dalí dressed and acted very unconventionally. His peers, confused and unsettled by his odd behavior, threw stones at him while his schoolteachers feared he was mentally impaired. His bewildered parents had no idea how to guide young Salvador's creativity and projected onto him their feelings about his older brother, also named Salvador, who had died just prior to Dalí's birth. His late brother had been very well behaved and obedient, and his parents expected the same behavior from him, but the young Salvador Dalí was never able to come remotely close to their ideal. Instead, he defied them by indulging in hyperactive, eccentric behavior. Once, the young Salvador brought a dead bat to school and bit into it, and then jumped down a flight of stairs in front of his schoolmates. He claimed that this was his way of expressing "my unusualness," as he called it (Hillman 1997).

Fortunately, Dalí was eventually able to harness his extreme need for creative stimulation and his passion for the unusual, and express himself through art. In fact, many great artists—Mark Rothko, Andy Warhol, and John Lennon are just a few examples—have reported that in childhood, they felt like outcasts because of their differentness and that this influenced their artistic expression.

A person's "differentness" might seem quite ordinary compared to Dalí's but still inspire feelings of suspicion, resentment, and disapproval from those she cares about or from the people surrounding her. We resist actions that might cause others to perceive us as "strange," because we fear that if we don't conform to their expectations, we'll be lonely and suffer. One of my clients, Sam, was a teenager who was picked on at school and mocked by the other children, because they felt he dressed oddly and behaved strangely. It was difficult for him to see that even as they ridiculed him, their behavior was rooted in their own insecurities. Sam's parents themselves were iconoclasts and encouraged Sam to embrace his unusualness, but being an adolescent, Sam wanted to feel accepted by his peers. I helped him to recognize that many young people, if not the ones in his school, embraced his interests and that his style of dress, which was comfortable for him, could be altered in some ways to be more stylish without making him feel irritated by his clothing. I also helped him identify peers who perceived his "strangeness" as something positive. If Sam could let go of his desire to fit in with everyone else and, instead, embrace his "unusualness," he wouldn't create so much emotional suffering for himself and would open himself up to relationships with peers who could accept him.

Often, even as adults, we'll cling to the desire to fit in with everyone else, at the expense of our own imagination. If we can recognize that our resistance is rooted in the false belief that being different will automatically result in loneliness and suffering, we can start to accept who we are and create relationships with people who aren't unsettled by or envious of us. By acknowledging and facing our fear of our uniqueness and ingenuity, we mine our own gold and discover our originality. As we step into this new role of power and passion, we'll naturally and easily attract an entirely new and supportive community of friends and colleagues.

PAYOFF 3: WE CAN AVOID FAILURE. Heinz Kohut, considered the grandfather of psychology of the self, said that the fear of failure is intimately connected to our childhood fear that if we risk behaving in a new way, our parents or primary caretakers will be angry and withdraw from and abandon us, leaving us feeling helpless, needy, and dependent. When we fear failure, we tend to overestimate the risk we're taking and imagine the worst possible scenario—the emotional equivalent of our parents deserting us as children. What we picture is so dreadful that we convince ourselves that we shouldn't even try to change. We avoid opportunities for success, and then, when we fail, our mantra is "Success just isn't written in my stars."

Our distorted beliefs about how great a risk we're taking and how bad the outcome can turn out to be usually originate in our past. Over the years, we tend to embellish the story of a failure until it's deeply painful for us to remember it. Overcoming the fear of failure requires us to consciously examine our long-forgotten experiences of feeling embarrassed or ashamed after taking a risk, and put them into perspective. Otherwise, the layers of embarrassment and shame can leave us feeling that taking *any* risk, no matter how small, is dangerous and terrifying.

I recall two shameful experiences of public speaking that instilled in me a tremendous fear of ever addressing an audience again. First, when I was six years old and in the first grade, I needed a minor operation to clip the skin that connected the bottom of my tongue to the bottom of my mouth; the goal was to eliminate my tongue-tiedness, making it easier for me to speak. The surgery was performed shortly before the school year began, and I ended up missing the first week of class. On my first day back, my new teacher thought it would be a great idea for me to stand up in front of the class and share my experience of the operation with my schoolmates. Needless to say, when I began to speak with my still-swollen tongue, I stuttered and slurred all of my words while my classmates taunted and jeered at me. My face turned red from embarrassment, pain, and shame. I vowed I would never again speak before a group of people if I could possibly help it.

A few years later, my Boy Scout leader noticed that I avoided any situation where I would have to speak in front of an audience, and encouraged me to be the troop scribe, which required that I read the minutes from the previous meeting. This small step toward overcoming my fear and insecurity inspired me to join the Toastmasters International club when I was fifteen. One day, as part of a public-speaking contest, I had to give a ten-minute speech without notes. The rule was that if you forgot your speech or lost your place, you couldn't leave the stage. My team was counting on me, and my nervousness mounted as I unconsciously remembered my earlier, traumatic experience from many years before. Seven minutes into my presentation, I forgot what I'd intended to say. I stood frozen with horror, desperate to recover my train of thought. Two minutes passed that felt like twenty as shame and humiliation overcame me. A team member in the audience gave me the thumbs up, and instantly, I remembered what I'd planned to say and was able to continue, but my confidence was shaken again. The incident had reinforced my belief that if I were to risk speaking publicly in the future, I would surely embarrass myself.

Several years later, during the Vietnam War, I was asked by one of the administrators at my college to give a speech at an antiwar demonstration being held to protest the killings of four students at Kent State University in Ohio by the National Guard. I was very flattered and excited at the thought of being able to express my sincere beliefs about the war and the Kent State tragedy. At the same time, I was extremely nervous, because I remembered my failures at public speaking in my childhood. They loomed large in my mind, and I'm sure my memory of the events became distorted by the intensity of my shame. Probably no more than three children giggled when I spoke as a first grader, but whenever I recalled that incident, it seemed that a roomful of people had roared with laughter at my failure.

I stayed up most of the night researching and preparing my speech, and the next day, I arrived at the school auditorium and discovered that it was overflowing with students and faculty. I took a deep breath and told myself that I'd already experienced the worst that could happen when speaking publicly, so I really had nothing to fear. I'd forgotten my words once and been ridiculed by an audience, but I had survived.

Although nervous, I spoke from the heart, and the audience met my passionate presentation with a standing ovation as well as shouts for the school to shut down and join the national boycott of the bombing of Cambodia. After all of the handshaking, hugging, and applause, I sat down and experienced the old fears of failure, shame, and embarrassment wash over me and gently pass out of my being.

Since then, I've given over a thousand public presentations that have filled me with excitement, and I've come to discover that to overcome the fear of failure, we have to acknowledge it, put it in perspective, and then go ahead and take that first fierce step into the unknown. When we do, we may actually discover that what was once a formidable challenge is now second nature. We can open ourselves up to possibilities that we would once have scoffed at. Certainly, as a teenager who'd overcome at least some of my fears about addressing an audience, I would never have believed that one day, I'd have a rewarding career that required a great deal of public speaking.

Many creative individuals have stories of crippling fear of failure that they could not completely erase but were able to overcome through being consciously aware of it and letting themselves experience it yet determinedly moving forward despite it. Performers George Harrison and Carly Simon have often spoken about their paralyzing stage fright, yet their desire to perform was so strong that they allowed themselves to become aware of the fear and walk onto a stage nevertheless. Michael Jordan has told the story of how he was cut from his junior-high-school basketball team for poor performance, and was reduced to gathering up the balls after practice and watching his peers from the sidelines. By getting in touch with his deep desire to play, he was able to overcome the obstacles that had kept him from performing well, and went on to become a legendary NBA player.

PAYOFF 4: WE CAN AVOID SUCCESS. Strange though it may seem, a fear of success can cause as much resistance to change as a fear of failure can. While you may consciously long for a promotion or hope that your romantic relationship will result in marriage, unconsciously you may be afraid of what will happen if these changes occur. You may fear that your friends and loved ones will envy your success and withhold their love and approval or even abandon you because they can't tolerate their feelings of jealousy and self-hatred. You may also be afraid that with success will come shame and embarrassment as jealous people try to sabotage you and pull you back down to their own level of achievement.

These fears aren't completely unfounded. It's unfortunate that many people can't appreciate and applaud the triumphs of others, and that rather than being inspired to actualize their own talent or creativity, they allow the acorn of their greatness to lie dormant as they focus their energies on tearing down other people. We see people acting out their anger and jealousy when celebrities experience something embarrassing, the public scoops up tabloids that promise to reveal the salacious details, and gossip columnists revel in portraying them in the worst possible light.

However, even people who aren't famous suffer from the destructive behavior of those who envy them. A client of mine named Richard was devastated when his boss told him that despite his impressive streak of signing talented new artists whose projects were selling well, he would note in Richard's personnel records that he needed to tone down his boisterous communication style. He claimed that Richard's coworkers thought less of him because he was "too loud." Richard later learned that his coworkers felt and had expressed no such thing, but his boss's discomfort with his rising star had caused him to feel the need to make Richard feel inferior. His boss's words were very powerful, because in fact, Richard had always been insecure about his communication style, for which he'd been ridiculed in his youth.

You don't have to let your fears of the very real pitfalls of success hold you back if you allow yourself to become aware of your own, hidden insecurities and bring them to the light of consciousness. Then, you can examine them and consciously choose to assign them no value.

At the root of the fear of success is the darkness of low self-worth. When the self attempts to implement change, internal demons emerge like hounds from hell to attack, and in our fear, we create the thought, "Who am I to deserve comfort, safety, and a sense of well-being?" Feelings of shame and embarrassment arise, and all the energy that could be used to create something new gets used to attack and criticize the self.

If you can muster the courage to face your insecurities, you can heal yourself of the shame that prevents you from soaring to your destiny. Becoming aware of your insecurities also helps you see when others are acting out of envy, fear, or anger, and that makes it easier for you to consciously reject their distorted and hostile criticism.

PAYOFF 5: WE CAN AVOID FEELING GUILTY. If we take a risk and make a change, we may feel guilty because we're contradicting what others think we should or shouldn't be doing with our lives. For example, sometimes when a woman makes the choice to focus on a high-powered career track rather than on getting married and having children, the people she cares about may express feelings of hurt, disappointment, and anger that she's made this choice, while those who aren't close to her may judge her as psychologically imbalanced or lacking in some way. It takes great courage to stay true to the soul's calling when it's in conflict with what others believe we should want for ourselves.

To embrace the art of creative transformation, you must work through any feelings of guilt stemming from the belief that if you attempt to express your unique individuality and agenda, you're being bad or selfish. Attending to yourself differs from being selfish. You're only selfish if you take advantage of others for your own gain or knowingly cause them to suffer while giving no thought to whether you could prevent their being hurt.

When you feel guilty about pursuing your life's purpose or moving in a new direction, your mind can cause your body to feel pain or discomfort. You may have difficulty sleeping, or experience an overall sense of tension, anxiousness, depression, or chronic irritability. The fear of saying yes to yourself and no to others can bind with feelings of guilt and anxiety. To break the paralyzing chains of guilt, you must consciously identify the old messages and beliefs that create that emotion. Listen to the wisdom of your body, which often knows that something's wrong before your conscious mind does. Often, people who've experienced regular migraine headaches, backaches, and gastrointestinal problems that medications couldn't quite control are stunned when these problems vanish after they leave a bad relationship or an unfulfilling job, break the chains of guilt, and set sail into the unknown.

If you follow the compass of your own heart's desires, your own passions and goals, you may well disappoint others, but you shouldn't deny your soul's needs in order to please the people around you. In fact, if you do, you're likely to find that those you were so eager to placate still disapprove, because their dissatisfaction is rooted in their own low self-esteem, which you can't affect. Parents who deeply disapprove of their children have a highly critical streak inside them, as well as an inner sense of emptiness and a feeling of disconnection from their true selves. For these parents, nothing their children do is ever good enough, and they harbor feelings of anger, disappointment, and resentment. Once you accept that there's no path so sunny, so free of underbrush that you'll experience no suffering or discomfort as you walk it, you'll find it easier to open up to the full force of your passion and let it guide you despite others' condemnation of your choices.

You must have faith in yourself and your purpose if you're going to continue following your inner compass that guides your ship of self even when you experience the unexpected along the way. If you take the journey, you'll be able to look back without regret and know that you took the path you were meant to take. You'll understand that opportunities for growth and happiness lie in the most unexpected places along the way, ready to be seized if you're open to recognizing and embracing them. I don't believe we ever *get over* a significant loss, but we do learn to *move through* it and live with it, and perhaps even learn to use it creatively to find our life's purpose as well as harvest its lessons.

When you give in to hidden fears of the unknown, of appearing odd, of failing, or of succeeding, or when you're resisting change in order to avoid guilt, it's hard to believe that the discomfort and pain of accepting or making changes is worth experiencing. Your suffering may be so great that it feels as if it'll never dissipate. However, after a loss, something new will come into your life, and it may well be something of equal or greater value. For Mark and Selena, the parents of the children killed in the car crash, the challenge was to let go of their identity as noble, good, grieving parents and the idea that if they were to move forward, they would somehow hurt their children or prove themselves to be selfish. Only in letting go of these beliefs and feelings could they begin to create a new life, both as individuals and as part of their family.

Identify and Accept Your Resistance

The first step in letting go of your resistance is to identify what it is. As you work through the program in this book, you'll come to appreciate how using mindfulness and the creative process of change allows you to let go of these powerful roadblocks. In fact, once you stop putting tremendous effort into resisting change, you'll find that you've unharnessed a great deal of energy, formerly used to repress your painful feelings. This energy will propel you forward to where you want to go. First, however, you must uncover, experience, and accept the painful truth of why you're fighting so hard to hold on to your resistance.

Take the time to answer the following questions, writing your answers in your mindfulness journal. Close your eyes and allow images and sensations to come from you. These may be images from your past; for example, as a teenager, when I thought of public speaking, I could see myself standing in front of my first-grade class with all the students looking at me, and I could feel that my tongue seemed heavy, an image and sensation that created a strong feeling of fear in me. I also imagined that as I stood in front of a new audience, I would fail again to speak well, and I could imagine someone in the front row placing his hand in front of his mouth to hide his chuckling. While it's painful to allow these images, sensations, and emotions to arise in your mind, it's an important part of the process of recognizing, or being mindful of, what your fears are and where they're coming from. Take your time with each of these questions:

1. Why are you afraid to move forward toward what you say you want in life? What are your fears? Where are those fears coming from? What memories of past experiences are creating the fear? What future are you envisioning that causes you to feel fearful about these possibilities?

2. Are you afraid of any of the following? Take your time answering, and allow your mind to focus on these ideas. Open yourself up to any images or sensations that arise as you focus your thoughts on these common areas of resistance:

    ❧ The unknown, having a new experience of life

    ❧ Being perceived as too different or even strange

    ❧ Failing, suffering disappointment, or losing something of value

    ❧ Achieving success; increasing your visibility, financial status, or prestige; being noticed by others who may not have noticed you before

❧ Feeling guilty because you've disappointed people who care about you, believe in you, or have invested in you; feeling like a fraud or guilty over the thought that you've achieved something that you had no right to achieve or that your achievement takes away from someone else's happiness

Often, resistance creates sensations or feelings within the body that need to be discovered and dissolved. The Sweeping Body Meditation is an excellent tool for ridding yourself of them.

Sweeping Body Meditation

Sit comfortably and bring your attention to your breath, and then to the top of your head. Focus your awareness on what you're experiencing. Try to locate three sensations or feelings within your body. Allow yourself to become aware of them. Identify the quality of each. Do you feel a hot or cold sensation? One that's throbbing or sharp, rigid or fluid?

As you breathe in, imagine that the air you inhale is infusing that area of your body, cleansing and healing it. As you exhale, breathe out the quality of that sensation. So, if you have a burning pain in your shoulder, breathe in, imagining a coolness entering your shoulder, and breathe out, feeling the burning sensation flowing out of you. Feel your abdomen expanding and contracting as you move air in through your nostrils, into your lungs, and into the area of your body you're focusing on, and then out of your body, carrying with it the sensation you hope to heal. See the healing air coming in and the negative quality being swept out of you as you inhale and exhale. Continue for as long as you feel is necessary.

You might also want to envision a very warm, healing hand entering into your body where you're experiencing discomfort, and touching all the particles of pain, gathering them up as you inhale and scattering them outside of you as you exhale. Another option is to visualize your body as similar to that of an infant who has just come out of the bath and is wet. As you breathe in and out, visualize a soft, fluffy towel patting your head, face, neck, shoulders, and so on down to your toes and fingers. Let the towel

absorb all the unpleasant sensations in your physical body, until you experi-
ence a state of emptiness and freedom, and no longer feel any particular
sensation or emotion.

A core tenet of Buddhism is that suffering is impermanent. As you get in touch with your fear and resistance, and accept it, be aware that this suffering will pass away. You'll start to remedy any uncomfortable feelings, beliefs, and sensations by embracing positive ones that will propel you through the process of change, which you'll learn about next.

CHAPTER 5

Let Go of Destructive, Unwholesome Beliefs and Emotions

*My life belongs to the whole community and as long as I live
it is my privilege to do for it whatsoever I can. I want to be
thoroughly used up when I die, for the harder I work, the more
I live. I rejoice in life for its own sake. Life is no "brief candle"
to me. It is a sort of splendid torch which I have got hold of for
the moment; and I want to make it burn as brightly as possible
before handing it on to future generations.*

—George Bernard Shaw

In Buddhist psychology, we recognize three categories of emotions, feelings, and thoughts: positive (wholesome), neutral, or negative (unwholesome). Anything with an unwholesome quality causes suffering, so we try to remedy or replace these destructive, afflictive thoughts and feelings with their wholesome counterparts.

Acceptance of what's happening in the moment, and of the current situation, is a cornerstone of Buddhism. The paradox is that this wholehearted acceptance of the present, regardless of how unpleasant or even painful circumstances might be, is absolutely necessary if you're to change the situation for the better. From acceptance, you move into action. When you're resisting what is, you blind yourself to the possibilities of what might be. When you accept what is, you experience spaciousness and expansiveness, and ideas and creativity rush in. Opportunities present themselves. You can embrace them and move forward with wholesome, productive actions that are in harmony with what you hope to achieve. You'll feel energized and vitalized instead of being dragged downward by fear and pessimism. However, this turn toward wholesome thought, feeling, and action can only occur after you've shed your resistance and accepted the present circumstances.

As you meditate mindfully, generating the beneficial remedies recommended in this chapter, you may find it difficult to be accepting. If you're experiencing ambivalence or resistance to this antidote, explore that response after you leave the meditation cushion, either on your own, through writing in your mindfulness journal or self-reflection, or with a therapist or health professional.

Destructive attitudes about confidence, sensuality, ambition, and other wholesome qualities, along with unwholesome beliefs, may be hidden in your unconscious mind. If so, they can only be discarded if they're brought into conscious awareness and examined. For example, I've worked with clients who found it difficult to generate a feeling of confidence or ambition, because they were taught that only arrogant, self-centered, or shallow people experience those feelings. Those who were abused in the past often have difficulty allowing themselves to feel confidence and trust because of painful memories of betrayal and deeply embedded fear and distrust. These areas of hidden resistance to particular wholesome qualities will remain deep within until they're consciously deconstructed and reformulated.

In Buddhist psychology, the thought is said to be the seed that creates emotion, which in turn creates a feeling or sensation. The ever-active mind will add to this sequence, layering on new thoughts and emotions that are equally unwholesome. To stop this buildup of negativity that causes increased suffering, we can apply a wholesome remedy to the afflictive quality at any place in that sequence. Then, later, we can take the time to fully explore our unconscious, unwholesome beliefs.

ADDRESSING AFFLICTIVE THOUGHTS

Cognitive behavioral therapy, also known as *cognitive therapy*, is a very effective approach to dealing with painful, afflictive thoughts, which are often based in habits of the mind and, upon examination, reveal themselves to be quite distorted and unwholesome. When these thoughts arise, you don't have to continue your narrative of suffering. Instead, you can stop, observe what you're thinking, and ask yourself, "Is this true?" You can consider the evidence that it is and weigh that against the evidence that it isn't, keeping in mind that extreme statements such as "I'll never..." or "It always happens that..." are almost certainly distortions. Using logic and reason, you can analyze a situation and determine whether you were assuming a worst-case scenario, and consider what the best-case scenario and even the most likely scenario are. This type of unemotional analysis provides perspective that allows for retraining the mind. You set aside the instantaneous, distorted, unwholesome thoughts and embrace more positive, wholesome ones, laying new neural pathways and building mindstrength. If you don't know whether a particular negative thought is likely to be true, you can explore the possibilities instead of being pessimistic and assuming the worst.

The next step in examining an unwholesome thought is to replace it with one that's wholesome. Working with a mindfulness trainer or a therapist can be very helpful for figuring out specific wholesome, remedying thoughts. You may choose to write out these replacement thoughts, which can be very effective. However, when you first begin using this remedy of a positive thought, feeling, or sensation, you're likely to feel resistance, as the old neural pathways in the brain protest, "But this isn't true!" One way to get around this obstacle is to design remedying thoughts that feel true in the moment. Instead of trying to replace an unwholesome feeling of longing and emptiness with the belief, "I'm going to meet the love of my life very soon," you can remedy that afflictive feeling with a thought such as "I'm doing all the right things to attract and create a healthy, loving partnership," which is less likely to arouse feelings of dishonesty, discomfort, or embarrassment. The emotional response to this wholesome, remedying thought needs to be positive for it to take hold in the mind and body, and begin to lay a new neural pathway in the left-prefrontal cortex. Otherwise, you can achieve the opposite effect, creating even more negative thoughts and feelings instead of remedying the ones your mind has already churned up. In mindfulness training, the key is for the meditator to notice the direction of the mind flow in every moment and redirect it when it's moving toward unwholesomeness. You actually teach the mind to create wholesome thoughts, and in so doing, you reprogram your brain, replacing old neural networks with new ones that foster creativity and optimism.

Once you've generated this positive and healing thought, you can make a point of saying the words silently or aloud every time you witness yourself thinking negatively. Let's say you're experiencing the recurring negative thought, "I'm no good with numbers, so I can't go into business or handle my finances by myself without my late spouse to guide me." First, you need to look at the evidence that you're "no good with numbers." It may be that higher-level math is difficult for you, but you're comfortable with basic adding, subtracting, multiplying, and dividing. Look back to the source of that belief, examining your past: Were you good at math in high school but not at applying and using it in your personal life? Is there evidence that you have no aptitude for numbers, or does it simply feel that way because you never quite learned how to balance a checkbook? Is it possible that you can address this shortcoming? Perhaps you're not good at organizing receipts and keeping track of spending, and not quite sure why your checkbook doesn't always balance out. A few new skills and the right software programs might do a lot to change your belief, "I'm no good with numbers." You may simply need to notice that your mind is creating a negative loop of self-talk, comprised of self-defeating thoughts. By adopting the new, wholesome thought, "I'm fully capable of learning anything I wish to learn," your mind flow will begin to shift and travel on a more wholesome course.

Because we shut down our creativity at an early age, often we become quickly convinced that if we don't already know something, we can never learn it. The belief "You can't teach an old dog new tricks" has been shown to be false, at least as far as brain science is concerned. The brain is far more malleable than ever thought. We can develop relationship, communication, and money-management skills. There may be many ways of solving problems and getting around roadblocks we haven't thought about, from outsourcing to technology. Once we remedy our unwholesome and limiting beliefs, we open up to a greater range of possibilities accessible through open mind, the doorway to our deepest, or core, creativity.

Often, unwholesome, painful thoughts are about the past and the future, or cause and effect: You might think, "If I wasn't able to do that in the past, I won't be able to do that in the future" and "Because of what I did in the past, I can't create the future situation I'd like." Again, by applying mindfulness training, you open a doorway to a mindful-inquiry process in which you can examine these beliefs and let go of a sense of being stuck or trapped. Painful and fearful thoughts about the past and future will prevent you from focusing on the present, and accepting where you are at this moment in time. If you need to move to the West Coast in order to pursue your dream career, a thought such as "I've failed so many times in my life that I shouldn't take this risk" or "I won't be able to make it in such a highly competitive field" prevents you from looking clearly at where you are now and what you might need to do before making such a move. It may be that you're fully capable of achieving your future goal, but if you can't face your present situation with honesty and creativity, you won't be able to remedy your unwholesome thoughts, feelings, and sensations, and move forward.

We can also have fearful thought patterns about the present that create obstacles that constrict and imprison us within the limitations of our unwholesome thoughts and feelings. Starbucks wouldn't exist if its corporate leaders had believed, "People don't like coffee enough to pay three-fifty for a cup of it" or "People only drink coffee from diners; they'd have no interest in a store that sells only coffee"—or, if later they'd thought, "People who love coffee don't want to buy tea" or "People who love music don't want a corporation recommending music to them." Such massively successful companies can't continue to exist if their creative leaders don't continually find new ways to compete in the marketplace. When we're able to experience expansiveness, we tap into an infinite number of possibilities.

Creative individuals have learned the habit of rejecting limiting, constrictive thinking. They allow the witnessing mind to arise, look at an obstacle, and say, "Perhaps that's true, but let's sit with that idea for a while." With mindfulness training, you'll find it natural to entertain the impossible and even the absurd. You can let go of the constricting belief that it's a waste of time to consider new ideas that seem unworkable or that have "already been done" and, instead, open up to new possibilities that reveal themselves. In Buddhism, we say that a constrictive quality of mind keeps mind flow within a narrow range of awareness, while mindfulness allows us to drop our limitations and ultimately enter the creative space of open mind.

The doves that remained at home,   never exposed to loss,
innocent and secure,   cannot know tenderness;
only the won-back heart   can ever be satisfied: free,
through all it has given up,   to rejoice in its mastery.

—Rainer Maria Rilke, "Dove That Ventured Outside"

Addressing Unwholesome and Painful Emotions

The mindstrength you develop through the practice of mindfulness will give you the courage to address even the most painful, unwholesome emotions, allowing you to bring them into your conscious awareness, experience them, and let them go so that you can redirect your mind toward more wholesome ones. As you sit with what is, and bring mindful awareness to it moment by moment, spontaneously and without effort, you may feel your unwholesome emotions and sensations transforming into more wholesome ones without your needing to bring in the wholesome remedies.

Sometimes, you'll feel the need to push aside your grief lest it overwhelm you with its intensity. This is understandable, but the longer you avoid your pain and attempt to push it away, the more difficult it will be to break out of paralysis. Just as birds are drawn to bread crumbs on the ground, the pain will keep returning to you after you shoo it away. Buddhism teaches that as you sit with your pain and grief, simply noticing it as if you were sitting on a riverbank watching your feelings float downstream, you'll discover how to live, learn, and heal through it.

Another helpful tool for transitioning through loss is to envision yourself going through the experiences of someone else who has been in a situation like yours and was successful at putting the pain and heartbreak behind him. *Cinematherapy* and *bibliotherapy* can be useful tools for vicariously experiencing the suffering and triumph of someone else and developing the courage to begin your own similar journey. In these forms of therapy or self-therapy, you watch a movie or read a book that touches upon the themes in your own life, and allow yourself to experience any emotions, thoughts, or sensations that come up in response to what you're viewing or reading. Afterward, you ponder the parallels between what happened on-screen or on the page and what's happening in your own life.

The feelings that arise when you let yourself slow down, become quiet, and access what's in your heart can be overwhelmingly intense. Years ago, after I reluctantly ended a romantic relationship with a woman I'd considered to be the perfect match for me, I was left feeling so empty, lost, abandoned, distraught, and filled with despair that no matter what I talked about in therapy or with friends, nothing about the pain seemed to shift. I had what felt like an eternal sense of emptiness and despair. After months of suffering, I decided to check myself in to a ten-day mindfulness retreat. Every moment of the day, from sunup to sundown, every thought, every sensation in all of my cells, and every nerve in my body ached. At my lowest emotional point, I experienced a series of endless thoughts that the best way to end the pain might be to quietly go off into the desert like a sick or wounded animal and die. It seemed that everybody else in the meditation hall was in bliss, but here I was, an esteemed and highly trained clinician and student of mindfulness, wrestling with such dark, bleak, and lonely thinking. It was then that the following healing meditation came to me.

Broken-Heart Recovery Meditation

Relax and gently sit on your meditation cushion or in a sturdy, straight-back chair (if you have back pain, lie down on a solid floor), and begin to notice your inhalation and your exhalation. As your breath brings more and more comfort to you, and you can notice that your lungs are supporting your brain with more and more oxygen, settle deeply into that space of mindful relaxation and exploration. Go now to your heart and feel the pain, emptiness, or sadness. Breathe deeply and bring mindful awareness to the suffering within your heart.

You may become surprised and delighted to discover that while you're simply noticing your grief or sorrow and experiencing compassion for yourself, a wondrous mind flow has begun. Like ice melting in the mountains, pain and sorrow ebb away, flowing out of your heart and your body, out from your feet and hands. Continue to breathe and allow these powerful and painful feelings, sensations, and thoughts to move through you and out of you.

If your suffering isn't alleviated, allow yourself to become curious and imagine someone who suffered terribly and overcame her loss, someone whose story you know well. Picture this person in your mind's eye and take yourself through her story of loss and pain from its inception in all its intensity and agony. Place yourself inside her heart, mind, and body. Allow yourself to feel every feeling, and experience each and every dark moment and mood you imagine she suffered. Draw strength from her tragedy and triumph. Visualize and bring mindful awareness to the exact moment in her mind when she made the decision to heal, to transform the direction of pain and sorrow in order to move from internalization to expressive flow. See, feel, and experience yourself as this person as she drew strength, wisdom, and compassion from this heartache.

Envision your heart and imagine the tissue within its wounds begin to repair itself. Feel a stirring of vitality as your heart beats and you imagine seedlings in the earth beginning to awaken from dormancy and buds on the branches of trees beginning to open to the sunlight as flowers burst forth with a new aliveness and energy.

Notice that your heart and mind are beginning to transform. Be mindful of the feelings in your heart as you draw from your inner resource of compassionate awareness. Notice the loss, sorrow, and sadness beginning to shift toward feelings and sensations of vitality, passion, and well-being.

By recreating in your own mind someone else's pain *and* subsequent recovery, you may find yourself feeling less overwhelmed and better able to avoid getting caught up in an unwholesome series of thoughts, feelings, and sensations. You can also try envisioning yourself going through a series of steps to move from emotional depletion to recovery, a process of combining mindful awareness with core creative resources available to you in your unconscious mind. However, that can be more difficult to do, because the mind has to access creativity to give you some idea of how your life might unfold in the days to come. Your grief or anger may be too powerful for you to enter a creative state, so it may be easier to pretend to be this person who has successfully navigated her transformation.

MINDFULNESS AND PAIN

Some bodily sensations are mild, and serve to awaken us to unwholesome thoughts and beliefs we're holding in parts of our bodies, such as "sensation of weakness in my back" or "constriction in my belly." Other sensations are very strong and can be rooted in a physical ailment. Chronic pain or the pain caused by an acute illness can be so distracting and intense that it becomes extremely difficult not to let the mind generate depressive, pessimistic thoughts and feelings.

Mindfulness practice can significantly reduce the chain of anger, despair, and sorrow caused by chronic pain. It can also help uncover any hidden, unwholesome products of the mind that contribute to, or even cause, that pain. Years ago, just after a series of losses I thought I'd put behind me emotionally, I was in a skiing accident and was told that it was possible I'd torn my rotator cuff.

For over a year, I underwent treatments from physical therapy to acupuncture to immobilizing my shoulder but got no relief from my chronic pain. I was considering surgery when a dharma (which, in Buddhism, means "the way" or "the path of enlightenment") teacher of mine suggested I meditate on my shoulder pain to fully enter it and sit with it, simply observing it while experiencing it. I entered a meditative state and became fully focused on the aching sensation, when suddenly I was overcome with grief and began to sob uncontrollably. I wept copiously for what must have been an hour, my chest heaving as I experienced the depths of my unprocessed grief. Gradually, the emotional pain subsided along with the physical pain. To my great surprise, I never again felt pain in that shoulder. When I went back to my orthopedic surgeon, a fellow yoga practitioner, he said, "Sometimes we heal an injury from the inside out. Yours was a miraculous recovery!"

Not everyone will receive full relief from pain by bringing to the surface of their awareness any psychological issues that might be contributing to it. I caution my clients not to overanalyze their illnesses in the hope of discovering some magic key to curing their cancer, fibromyalgia, or back pain by bringing to the surface old memories and finally letting go of them. For some people, examining, identifying, and addressing possible psychosomatic causes may result in some relief, but not all pain or disease is psychosomatic, and the guilt generated by the question, "How did I manifest this illness?" is extremely counterproductive.

Besides, there are genetic and environmental reasons behind much of our physical suffering. When it comes to knowing the true source of why some people develop serious illnesses, we sometimes have insight into the underlying cause but, more often than not, are humbled by the mystery, the uncertainty, and the suffering. With mindfulness practice, we can learn to accept the reality of our situation instead of cause ourselves even more pain by feeling frustrated or guilty that we can't fully heal ourselves through sheer willpower.

That said, mindfulness can be extremely helpful in dealing with pain or the physical discomfort of illness. The goal should be to fully experience the pain in meditation rather than resist it. As you allow the pain to reach its full intensity in your awareness, cultivate the witness who observes it from a distance, noting its presence without being absorbed by it. This will lessen the intensity of the pain. Then you can alleviate the pain further by remedying it with a positive sensation that you mentally create. Whether your pain is throbbing, stabbing, aching, or dull, mentally creating a sensation of dissolution can be helpful. If the pain has the quality of tightness or constriction, imagine a sensation of flow and movement as you focus on that area of the body.

As you mindfully meditate on the pain, remedying it through visualization and lowering its intensity, you may want to make a bargain with yourself about the use of pain medication. Tell yourself, "If I could get through the last fifteen minutes with this pain, I can go for a full hour." At the end of that hour, tell yourself, "If I was able to get through the last hour with that level of pain, I can make it to lunchtime," and so on, promising yourself pain medication but pushing yourself to go just a bit longer without it each time your "deadline" approaches. In this way, you may be able to wean yourself off of pain medication or at least lower the amount you need to use in order to experience relief.

One of my clients had a mastectomy due to breast cancer and was understandably angry and resentful at the loss. Before the cancer, she had thought of her breasts as sensual and attractive, and now she hated looking at her chest and felt disassociated from this area of her body. When she meditated mindfully, she became aware of these feelings, and I suggested that she apply the remedy of a wholesome sensation, creating in her chest a sensation that encapsulated beauty, sensuality, and health. She also underwent regular deep massage to help her feel more connected to a body that had, in her mind, "betrayed" her. After many months of these complementary approaches, her doctors told her that the amount of painful scar tissue that had formed around her reconstructive breast implant was minimal. I believe the combination of mind-and-body healing methods she chose to use resulted in a reduction of her physical pain, while her mindfulness meditation practice helped rebalance her emotions and state of mind.

FIVE HINDRANCES AND THEIR REMEDIES

Buddhism recognizes hindrances, or combinations of feelings, sensations, and thoughts, that share particular qualities and can be addressed with a corresponding remedy. There are five hindrances that I've found to be particularly common in the experience of resisting needed or inevitable change: the hindrances of wanting, illusory thinking, torpor, restlessness, and doubt. You may experience more than one of these hindrances at a time, and their remedies can overlap somewhat, but I find recognition of these hindrances very helpful for understanding how to replace the negative thoughts, emotions, and sensations that can keep us stuck in an unwholesome mind-set.

Hindrance 1: Wanting Mind

"Wanting mind" has the qualities of grasping or clinging. We cause ourselves suffering when we ache for something that lies out of our grasp or cling in vain to something that has already passed away. Sometimes, wanting mind involves tightly holding on to something negative: an unwholesome belief about how things ought to be or should have been, or an unwholesome emotion such as anger, sadness, or jealousy. Mindfulness practice helps us develop the capacity to see clearly exactly what we're attached to so that we can let go of it and end our suffering. The hidden areas of resistance that emerge into our awareness can be noted and examined later so that we can make the conscious choice to reject them.

In wanting mind, we feel that our current state of unhappiness could be cured if only we could have the money, job, relationship, recognition, or power we had and lost, or never had and strongly desire. Wanting mind has the qualities of:

- longing, wishing, pining, yearning

- hunger or cravings

- sexual desires, cravings, or addictions

- greed, emptiness, and constant wanting

- envy or jealousy, competitiveness

- ill will or anger

- contempt

- resentment

- vengefulness

- an aversion to losing control and having to surrender the will of the ego

You can never completely avoid wanting mind or any other hindrance. Desire is part of being human. It causes us to strive toward bettering our lives and our world, and has led to many of the discoveries and inventions that have provided us with a higher quality of life. Yet despite all that we can achieve and possess, we can become convinced that we won't be happy or contented unless we acquire even more. This unwholesome belief can lead to competitiveness and feeling resentful toward, or envious of, those who seem to have an easier life.

When we're in a state of wanting mind, we're not satisfied, no matter what we have. If we attain the object of our longing, we simply replace the old desire with a new one. If we achieve revenge, we feel worse than we did before. The problem is that wanting mind is rooted in the incorrect belief that something outside of ourselves is the key to lasting happiness. The reality is that no emotion or state of being, however strong, is permanent and that happiness can't be found outside of ourselves, only within. Buddhists call this phenomenon of endless wanting and dissatisfaction the "hungry ghost."

For the most part, you can't control what happens as it occurs, but you have a choice about your mind. The decision to ride the wave of change helps you to accept your current circumstances and let go of any unwholesome thoughts or feelings your mind creates in response to the challenge. The more you build your mindstrength through mindfulness practice, the better your ability to maintain a sense of joy and contentment for long stretches before the wheel turns and the afflictions of sadness and anger arise again.

While working to remedy wanting mind, keep in mind that jealousy, envy, anger, and resentment are generated by false beliefs about yourself and others that are often rooted in early childhood, when mirroring takes place. If parents don't properly mirror their children's emotional reality, assuring them that their feelings are acceptable and temporary, children get the message that they must repress inconvenient, difficult feelings. Their longing to feel comfortable with their emotions distorts into a yearning for something external to assuage their pain. The child who feels ignored and unvalued desires toys, influence among his peers, or positive attention. These longings eventually develop into lust for material wealth, power, and fame, leading to competitiveness, jealousy, and resentment.

What we truly need in order to feel satisfaction is unconditional love for ourselves and self-acceptance. By focusing on what we don't have, we can become trapped in wanting mind, falling deeper into the dark hole of desire, unable to move forward and create a fulfilling life. Losses and crises can paralyze us as we agonize over the thought, "If only…"

The real antidote to suffering marked by the quality of wanting is not to achieve a temporary panacea but to experience satisfaction in this moment, exactly as it is. Only by experiencing satisfaction right now can you open yourself up to the type of creativity that will help you see what you have to do to bring about better circumstances. The following meditation can be used to replace feelings of envy and desire with the more wholesome feeling of satisfaction.

Satisfaction Meditation

Sit in a meditative posture, focusing on your breathing and saying "in" and "out" for each respiration for several minutes until you feel that you're in a state of calm mindfulness.

Visualize yourself sitting at a table with a large glass of clear, sparkling water before you. Feel your thirst, your lack, your wanting.

Reach for the glass and begin to drink from it. As you drink, this magic glass never empties. You feel the sensation of cool, satisfying water quenching your thirst as you drink. Drink with deep, satisfying gulps until you feel sated.

Now, become aware of a beam of warm, energizing light, a light of infinite knowledge and wisdom, shining all around you and infusing you with all that you'll ever need to know. Radiate in this light of wisdom, becoming one with it.

As you experience the sensation of being satisfied, feel yourself glowing with white light. Know that you are an illuminating beacon, shining brilliantly with the light of wisdom, love, and acceptance. Feel it inside of you, radiating outward. You have more than enough light inside of you. Experience it. Notice what it feels like to be satisfied, to be so filled with light that it flows forth from you, giving you a deep sense of satisfaction.

Remain present with this feeling of satisfaction until you're ready to open your eyes and end your meditation.

An alternative image you may want to use during this meditation is that of stretching your treelike roots downward, breaking through hard soil to reach the sustenance of groundwater deep in the earth. Again, imagine yourself drinking in all that you need until you are satisfied.

Addressing the underlying, distorted beliefs that lead to envy and jealousy is another important aspect of remedying wanting mind. Often, I've found that younger people put tremendous pressure on themselves to succeed in their careers at a very early age, not allowing themselves to venture out and explore, take risks, make mistakes, discover their talents and passions, and slowly begin formulating a plan for their personal mandala. One client, in particular, who dreamed of being a successful novelist, became deeply envious of a talented writer who'd written several best-selling novels that had defined a genre and made her famous. This client, who was only a year or two out of college, had managed to procure a scholarship to a prestigious writing program but felt disappointed in her inability to find a publisher for her novel.

Using mindfulness, this conflicted young woman was able to explore her belief that she should have as much skill and success as someone who had spent many years honing her craft and building her profile among booksellers and readers. In meditation, she recognized that she'd been repressing unwholesome feelings of low self-worth. I helped her see that the passion she was devoting to envying this best-selling author's success could be redirected to more productive activity if she would apply a positive antidote of satisfaction to her wanting mind, which had created a grandiose expectation completely out of proportion to a reasonable level of achievement for a writer just starting out.

Some people also have unrealistic expectations rooted in the narratives spun by popular culture. In movies and television shows, the difficulties of maintaining and nurturing relationships are often minimized in favor of a more engaging and unlikely story of couples who meet, fall in love immediately, have great sex as well as an unwavering long-term commitment, and rarely disagree—and if they do, they quickly resolve all their issues. The amount of effort and time that must be invested to foster a healthy relationship is often surprising to people with little experience of such relationships.

Wanting mind creates an unwholesome habit of comparison. Some people look at others' successes and feel deeply envious. They may be angry that they haven't achieved what they feel entitled to, start to diminish all that's working for them in their lives, and obsess over what seems to be lacking.

There's a danger in thinking that by ridding yourself of this quality of wanting, you'll lose the motivation to better your life. By dropping out of wanting mind and negative comparison, you'll drop into an acceptance of what's ordinary as well as what's extraordinary within yourself. Each of us has the potential to do something no one else has ever done before, and you open yourself to discovering just what that is when you replace wanting mind and its negative feelings and thoughts with a mind-set of satisfaction.

Hindrance 2: Illusory Perfection

Sometimes we dearly wish to hold on to a chimera: the illusion of perfection. You'll cause enormous suffering for yourself if you feel entitled to lasting satisfaction with every aspect of life. Thinking about what you "ought" to have achieved or acquired, you may become angry, frustrated, sad, or confused, wondering what went wrong. You may also find yourself feeling envious or jealous, thinking that the only thing standing between you and the perfect relationship, financial situation, career, or happiness is someone else.

The hindrance of illusory perfection has the qualities of:

- resentment

- anger

- frustration

- shock and bewilderment

- a desire to control the situation and make it perfect

The remedy for this hindrance is acceptance and clarity about the impermanent nature of your experiences. You'll vacillate between perfection and imperfection. Sometimes you'll get sick, lose stamina, or suffer a loss, but you can return to the sense of perfection at any time, regardless of what's happening.

In reality, no one's holding you back from experiencing perfection. It's the mind that conjures up the illusion that you can hold on to happiness, never experiencing pain. Every moment, no matter how perfect, must fade into the past. Another such moment can't occur until you let go of the hindrance of illusory perfection that keeps you locked in suffering.

To release the negative thoughts about your entitlement to perfection, you must let go of the idea that perfection is a set of unchanging, external circumstances that you find pleasing in every way. It's easy to be happy when your romantic partner is being nurturing and you're prosperous and successful, but as soon as the wheel turns, it's a struggle to maintain that state of joy. The illusion of perfection makes it even more difficult to feel a sense of acceptance and well-being. In fact, this illusion is particularly unwholesome, because it pulls you into wanting mind, regardless of how positive your actual circumstances are: every hairline fracture in your picture of perfection seems like a deep gash. The remedy is to accept whatever's happening in the present moment.

Imperfection Meditation

Breathing in and out, aware of each breath, imagine yourself wearing eyeglasses that allow you to see perfection in the world. You observe a sunset that's perfect in its beauty and grace. You look at the waves in the ocean or on a large lake and notice a perfect pattern of movement. You see an animal moving about in the woods, living in perfect harmony with its environment. You look at yourself interacting harmoniously with those you love. Pictures of your life come into your mind, and all are images of perfection. Feel the joy as you experience the beauty of perfection, everything working together, in perfect harmony, in perfect timing, in perfect relationship.

Breathe in and out, and let these pictures fade from your awareness. Become aware of your breath, in and out. You now are donning eyeglasses of imperfection. They allow you to see all the imperfection surrounding you. Allow the images of imperfection to arise into your awareness. Note what feelings come up for you as you see imperfection. Note how your body feels as you gaze upon the imperfections of the world, and observe the images that come into your mind.

You see with perfect clarity all the imperfections that surround you. Create a feeling of acceptance as you view all these imperfections with twenty-twenty vision. You can see every fracture, every flaw, every mistake, every injustice. You feel strong and accepting as you gaze upon each flaw that reveals itself to you. Everything is in a state of impermanence. You are merely gazing at a snapshot in time. Each imperfection is about to shift. Enjoy this perfect, clear snapshot of a split second in time: the present moment.

Hindrance 3: Sleeping Mind

Depression and ennui spring from the hindrance of "sleeping mind," which is marked by these qualities:

- drowsiness

- sluggishness

ᴥ fatigue

ᴥ laziness

ᴥ apathy

ᴥ malaise, or torpor

The remedy for sleeping mind is vitality, which is experienced in the body as well as in the mind. Vital thoughts and feelings arise when you awaken your body. To start remedying this hindrance, be mindful of any physical causes for your sluggishness, from a poor diet to a lack of exercise and sleep, and even allergies and intolerances to substances in your food and environment. Whenever a client has sleeping mind, I interview her at length about her health habits in order to ascertain whether the cause is the mind itself, or whether her torpor might be caused or influenced by a poor diet, food or environmental allergies, excessive use of intoxicants, lack of exercise, sleep disturbances, or too much stress (or a combination of these factors).

However, the mind and body influence each other, so stress and the powerful emotions of anger and sadness can create physical fatigue, which destroys motivation to move physically and leads to depressive thoughts and emotions. Exercise actually alters the body's chemistry, making it easier to let go of unwholesome states of mind and replace them with wholesome ones.

A major part of depression is the lack of energy or motivation to get out of bed, to do what needs to be done without procrastinating or giving in to the feeling that there's no point in taking action. To remedy torpor and depression, you have to experience the vital life force that sharpens the mind and focuses the awareness like a laser beam. The traditional Buddhist walking meditation focuses on the slow process of putting one foot in front of the other and being mindful of the shifting sensations as you propel yourself forward. In the following variation on a walking meditation, I've expanded the original exercise to encourage a reconnection with a sense of vitality and movement in the heart, lungs, and circulatory system.

Vitality Meditation

Find a place where you can walk that has minimal distractions so you can focus on your breathing and pay attention to what's going on inside of you. You might walk on a bike path or an indoor track, your living room floor, or even in an empty stairwell at the office. If you're going to walk out in nature, choose a grassy meadow or empty beach or path where you're unlikely to encounter many other people. Be sure to wear your most comfortable walking shoes and dress in clothing that will allow you to move easily. Remain silent throughout your walk, which should take at least ten minutes.

As you begin your walk, focus on your breath, mentally saying "in" on the inhale and "out" on the exhale. In a few minutes, refocus your awareness on your body. Feel your heel making contact with the ground. Feel your foot rolling forward and your weight shifting. Feel the ball of your foot pressing downward and the release of pressure as you roll off your toes and shift your weight to the heel of your other foot. Walk slowly so that you can be fully aware of these sensations you normally would ignore.

After a time, shift your awareness to your breathing and the feeling of oxygen coming into your lungs, being pumped through your heart and bloodstream, and reaching all the cells in your body. Feel the activity in your body at a cellular level, as each cell drinks in oxygen and your blood rushes to carry it to every cell in your brain, fingertips, chest, groin, thighs, calves, and toes. Feel your muscles strengthened by this oxygen. Feel your life force traveling through you, pushing you, propelling the blood through your veins and arteries. Feel your heart pumping steadily and reliably. Be aware of how the oxygen outside of you, always available to you, enters your body and surges through your organs and blood, mingling with your own life force.

Because sleeping mind can cause you to become isolated and begin generating unwholesome thoughts and feelings of loneliness, it can be helpful to do the vitality meditation with a friend or lover in order to feel a sense of support and connectedness. Walk together in silence.

Hindrance 4: Restlessness

On the surface, restlessness may seem like a positive state, because it inspires you to keep moving instead of becoming stagnant. Creative artists talk about having an "itch" or urge to get back into their music or art studio. What they're describing is a form of creative motivation that's quite different from restlessness. They're referring to a discomfort with being distracted and unfocused, and a desire to enter a focused, creative state.

Restlessness is good if it awakens you to a need to become meditative or immerse yourself in reverie. However, restlessness is most often simply undirected, unproductive action, such as puttering or flitting about from one activity to the next, never completing a task. As previously mentioned, in Buddhist psychology, we refer to this affliction of mind as "monkey mind."

Intuitively, most of us know that sitting down and meditating is a remedy for restlessness, but we resist this cure. A part of us knows that underlying the restlessness can be a cascade of negative thoughts and emotions that will cause us discomfort, and even pain, once brought to the surface. Thus, we give in to restlessness as a distraction and allow our minds to invent all sorts of excuses for our unproductive scurrying about.

The hindrance of restlessness has the following qualities:

- agitation

- distraction

- anxiety or panic

- depression

- procrastination

- anger

- mania

- a desire for intense or extreme pleasure

The hindrance of restlessness can be remedied with comfort and relaxation. Mindfulness meditation is likely to bring up to the surface of the water the churning thoughts and emotions that have been causing a disturbance from underneath, but after you've dealt with them, you can meditate on the remedy of comfort. Generating a feeling of comfort allows the mind's frenzied activity to slow down, and triggers the sympathetic nervous system to begin releasing calming hormones into the body and slow your heart rate and breathing.

The Comfort Meditation can be used as an antidote at any time, but it may be easier to perform after physical activity, which will also turn on the parasympathetic nervous system that counters the stress response. It's also particularly effective in conjunction with mindfulness meditation, which uncovers the source of restlessness so that it can be addressed.

Comfort Meditation

While sitting, breathing, and focusing on the inhale and the exhale, visualize yourself sitting at the edge of a beautiful blue lake where someone has just passed by in a motorboat. The wake from the boat sends ripples toward the shore. Watch as the froth at the top of the waves settles down in the distance and the choppy waters push toward you. Each wave becomes a little smaller, a little calmer, as it moves in your direction, toward shore. The motorboat is long gone. The waves smooth out as they reach the shore and become gentle ripples that spread quietly over the pebbles on the beach. You watch each tiny wave spread out over those pebbles until there's almost no movement from the water. You look out onto the lake and see how still it has become. The water is gently, almost imperceptibly undulating, growing ever more still.

Underneath the surface of the water, bits of sand and dirt that came in toward shore on the waves are now settling slowly to the bottom. All above and all below are still.

As you bring to the surface the products of the mind that are creating your restlessness, you may well find that they yield little of value or interest. A thought such as "With the economy in this state, I don't know how I'm going to stay solvent" is, in all likelihood, one that you've explored consciously but that your mind re-creates again and again in response to any situation that stirs up a feeling of fear or uncertainty. The well-worn pathways in the brain do an excellent job at efficiently producing the types of thoughts that will keep those highways open to many lanes of traffic. To find a new, less-traveled road takes conscious effort and the mindstrength to avoid the distraction of examining or reexamining every anxious thought generated in those established neural networks. Equanimity and comfort allow you to find the road to the core creativity that's available to you.

Hindrance 5: Doubt

The hindrance of doubt has the qualities of:

- skepticism

- cynicism

- confusion

- pessimism

The remedy for doubt is curiosity, appreciation of the mystery of life, and resolve, all of which are intertwined. Acceptance and wonder at the mystery, coupled with the resolve of acceptance, allows you to minimize the suffering of a loss. No one likes losing something of great value, and you don't have to believe the loss was meant to be part of a divine plan, although some may find that belief comforting. What's absolutely necessary is acceptance and the resolve to move forward with an open mind, believing that positive people, opportunities, and situations will show up in your life again.

You always have a choice of how to respond to unwanted change. Despite their popularity in our culture, cynicism and pessimism have been shown to be poor tools for creating a sense of well-being, although they may provide an illusory sense of power for a short time. The cynic who claims, "I know the system isn't set up to allow people like me to achieve my goals," isn't empowered but trapped in an unwholesome state of mind where his only choices are anger, sadness, and other unwholesome emotions. There can be no true joy or contentment in believing that what lies ahead will, in all certainty, generate more suffering.

Unlike pessimism, doubt at least leaves some room for the possibility of positive change. Mindfulness practice, which has been shown to build mindstrength and even increase the thickness in the area of the brain associated with optimism (Davidson et al. 2003), can help you avoid this destructive mind-set and the discomfort of confusion, which often leads to fear or depression.

During the worst suffering, you can cultivate the positive antidote of mystery, meditating on why tragedies must happen and how they interplay with triumphs. You can never know what your future sorrows or joys will be, but you can use your mindstrength to create the wholesome thought that positive circumstances will return to you because change is the nature of reality and, therefore, this too shall pass. Mystery, awe, and wonder will all connect you to your most innovative, resourceful self. Optimism allows you to trust that the vessel of wonder will take you through the fog to a hospitable land.

Hopefulness Meditation

Sitting comfortably, focusing on your in and out breaths, enter a state of deep mindfulness. Become aware of the solid ground underneath you. Become aware of your body and its strength. Be aware of your muscles that keep you upright.

Imagine that you're surrounded by clouds of many colors, all swirling gently around you. You can see nothing but pale, colored fog mingling with itself in front of your eyes. A bright, clear light begins to reveal an opening in the thick fog. With patience and acceptance, you sit contentedly, knowing that very soon, something positive will be revealed to you. You feel no need to push aside the clouds, which slowly part on their own. Experience hopefulness as you focus your awareness on this light, knowing that it's about to illuminate something wholesome and pleasing.

The impatience and desire to feel the comfort of knowing what lies ahead can cause you to become increasingly frustrated and give in to doubt. Like a professional athlete in the last quarter of a game in which her team trails by several points, you must remain in a state of hopefulness or openness and acceptance of the present moment. Focusing on what is, you can spot the opening that allows you to run the ball forward. But if you focus on failing to achieve your goals, you miss that opening.

Wholesome resolve and awe at the mystery provides a steadiness far more satisfying than the false security of pessimism and cynicism. To sit and look at the vastness of an ocean, the lushness of a mountainside covered with fir trees, or the swaths of stars in the night sky can help you to appreciate that you can never explain or explore every nook in the mystery of existence. Immersed in curiosity, you begin the art of creative transformation.

CHAPTER 6

Let Go of Unwholesome Self-Judgments

When there exists attachment,
contemplate impermanence,
unsatifactoriness,
and the No Self.

—Buddha

Many people cling to the myth that those who are successful inevitably feel good about themselves and are free from self-doubt and insecurities. Many clients I work with have résumés, personal achievements, and reputations that garner the deepest respect and admiration, yet their negative self-talk is often utterly brutal. Despite their low opinion of themselves, they've managed to fashion lives that many would envy. Yet the disconnection between their inner feelings about themselves and their outer success causes them to hold back from making changes that would lead to far greater fulfillment and equanimity. They'll often remain in a stagnant situation until change is thrust upon them, and then feel overwhelmed by the crisis they face.

One of the greatest obstacles to creative transformation is unwholesome self-judgments, and we all have them. The mind's ability to generate such judgments is very powerful, because it's working off old neural programming that must be rewritten again and again before new, more wholesome thought processes can become habitual. With more wholesome thought patterns in place, crisis becomes less overwhelming, and it's far easier to let go of resistance, tune in to your passions and inner resources, and move forward with confidence.

Becoming more insightful and reflective through mindfulness practice leads to greater awareness of the unwholesome self-judgments produced by your mind. You may be tempted to judge yourself as a bad meditator, or a failure at fixing your low self-esteem, but what you really are is a person making a long and sometimes arduous journey of self-discovery and self-acceptance. Don't hold yourself to unrealistic standards and expect to quickly transform what are often lifelong thinking habits.

The object is to stop assigning meaning to these self-judgments, because once you start to give them weight, they begin to weigh you down. Elaborating on these judgments will cause you to feel constricted by your unwholesome thought processes. Your ability to make breakthroughs, weather crises, and begin living more richly and more authentically will increase once you make a conscious decision to let go of unwholesome self-judgments every time you recognize them.

DISCOVERING AND BANISHING HIDDEN, UNWHOLESOME SELF-JUDGMENTS

Some self-judgments are neutral and don't create strong feelings of anger, joy, sadness, or excitement. They're simply part of your self-definition, and have no emotional baggage attached to them. For one person, the self-judgments "I'm energized by being around other people rather than by being on my own" or "I'm more comfortable in small groups than in larger ones" might not create any emotional response or inspire any disempowering stories about being extroverted or shy. Yet for another person, the very same self-judgments might elicit powerful emotional responses and extensive ruminating if they bubble up to the surface of awareness.

If you're not mindful, you may not notice when the thoughts, feelings, emotions, and sensations connected to a seemingly neutral self-judgment are unwholesome. Often, the rational mind strings together a series of distortions, such as "I'm shy, which is why I'll never find a romantic partner; my shyness makes me unattractive," or "I'm an extrovert. My mother never liked that about me, and it seemed to embarrass my siblings. I probably made a fool of myself many times, being too eager to connect to other people, who look down on me for being emotionally needy." You may not even be fully aware that you're embellishing your self-judgments in an unwholesome way.

Through mindfulness practice and self-inquiry, you can render any unwholesome self-judgments neutral and possibly even wholesome: being "self-centered," focused on resolving inner conflicts, can be seen as negative, but it's very important at times to direct your attention to yourself and your needs. For example, if you consider yourself to have the characteristic of "callousness," you might reframe it as the quality of courage. If you see yourself as "weak," consider perceiving yourself as being sensitive to other people's feelings.

You'll never rid yourself of your unwholesome self-judgments and be completely free from the suffering they cause you. However, you can alter their quality, learn from them, and either let them go or transform them so that they no longer block you from a sense of well-being, a feeling of spaciousness, and an openness to new possibilities. Most often, when you let go of your unwholesome self-judgments, you discover aspects of yourself that inspire and vitalize you. You start to have faith that you can live more authentically and richly.

A client of mine came to therapy because she was suffering badly from having been let go from several corporate positions and was now establishing herself as a freelance consultant. She had pervasive feelings of low self-esteem and a continual flow of unwholesome thoughts, such as "I can't earn a good living doing this, because no one will pay me what I was making before" and "Who am I to think I can run my own business?" Despite her obvious ability to procure good jobs, the fact that she had lost so many had shaken her sense of self-worth, even though several of her layoffs were due to corporate restructuring rather than to any failings on her part. Raised in a working-class home, she'd never quite felt she belonged at a major university, where she got her degree, or in a well-paying job with significant responsibilities.

We worked for quite a while to help her uncover and transform, or let go of, her unwholesome self-judgments and accept that there's an upside and a downside to every quality. Over time, she came to see that the perseverance that had led her out of her small town and to the big city, where she thrived, was still a quality she possessed. She was able to acknowledge how her perseverance had served her, as well as how it had held her back: when her companies had restructured or experienced financial difficulties, her unwillingness to recognize the need to look for a new position elsewhere and embrace the fact that change was in the air had resulted in her staying too long and being laid off. By mindfully accepting that she had the quality of "perseverance," which she realized could also take on unwholesome aspects and turn into stubbornness and rigidity, she was able to identify ways in which she might maximize its potential for her and minimize its negative effects. This allowed her to break apart the self-judgments she'd created, experience the flow of her inner resources and strength, and envision being a successful entrepreneur.

You may not realize that your unwholesome judgments of your qualities are holding you back from creative transformation. By tolerating the discomfort of examining your self-judgments and letting unwholesome thoughts, feelings, and sensations arise, you can drain them of their ability to frighten or stifle you. Turning them over to see their flip side allows you to see how you can embrace those qualities, consciously choosing to enhance their positive aspects and limit their negative effects. In a crisis, you can use the wholesome aspects of these qualities to propel you forward out of suffering.

The Most Painful Self-Judgments

Some of our self-judgments are so painful to acknowledge that we prevent our conscious mind from bringing them to the surface of our awareness. We sense that, like the visage of Medusa, they would create so much fear and anguish for us that we'd essentially turn to stone, unable to move out of our suffering. No one wants to face an excruciatingly painful thought such as "I'm a bad parent" or "Important people in my life don't respect me," yet such unwholesome and destructive beliefs about ourselves lie within many of us. Our fear magnifies danger out of all proportion.

By using mindfulness and the art of creative transformation, you can face the truth about yourself and hold on to faith that every one of your qualities can be mined for its beneficial aspects. Your deepest, or core, creativity, the fuel for the greatest breakthroughs in personal growth and transformation, will remain buried deep within your psyche until you acknowledge, examine, and then let go of the unwholesome self-judgments that obscure it.

Avoiding the Pain of Self-Discovery

Mindfulness practice breaks down avoidance behaviors, allowing hidden self-judgments to surface. We're often tempted to minimize their importance, in the vain hope of easing the pain of being aware of our "shortcomings." Often, my clients take pride in what they call their "self-honesty," reporting to me that they simply can't work for anyone else, that they have to be the boss, or that they're by nature aggressive and even offensive in their interactions with others and that can't be changed. Their bravado is an avoidance behavior. Underneath their false, external confidence is a fear that they *can't* work for anyone else, alter their behavior and take a more effective and nonaggressive approach, or interact with others in a positive, nonoffensive way.

The fear that you can't change may push you into denial and cause you to minimize the consequences of your unproductive behaviors. Whatever you discover about yourself and however painful your discovery, dramatic breakthroughs are always possible. Research on mindfulness meditation shows that qualities we once thought immutable that form temperament and character can actually be altered significantly. By retraining your mind through mindfulness practice, you create new neural networks. If you're aggressive, you can find ways to temper that aspect of yourself, becoming assertive and clear about your boundaries without entering into a competitive and possibly even hostile mind-set that will sabotage you. Even if you're a lifelong pessimist, you can learn to become more optimistic (Davidson 2000; Siegel 2007).

Working with Your Unwholesome Self-Judgments

As you've learned, the first step in dissolving any unwholesome thought, belief, judgment, emotion, or feeling is simply to watch it arise in your mind. Next, you identify it as wholesome, unwholesome, or neutral, and deal with it accordingly. If it's wholesome, savor it, experiencing it fully and drawing strength and joy from it. If it's unwholesome, come back to it during and after your meditation, and examine the mind patterns that generated it, consciously reshaping those patterns and then reinforcing your new ones through mindfulness practice. This process sounds simple, but you may find that the sensations and emotions accompanying your harsh self-judgments are so painful that you quickly find an excuse to end a session or, if you're not meditating, that you brush away what arises in your consciousness. Yielding to avoidance behaviors blocks the possibility of clearing up any unwholesome self-judgments.

Be assured that even if you were to discover that your unwholesome self-judgment has truth to it, simply making that painful discovery would take you a huge leap forward in your ability to transform that aspect of yourself. Your willingness to acknowledge this painful reality allows you to look at it more objectively and see that there are times when those judgments don't apply—and in fact, they may not apply most of the time. Knowing this can give you further confidence to accept that sometimes you exhibit unwholesome qualities, but you can change that disconcerting reality.

Everyone has qualities worthy of admiration and esteem that serve them well when harnessed. You'll be better able to claim yours and enhance them once you've done the important work of acknowledging, learning from, and letting go of your unwholesome self-judgments. You may want to begin this process by consciously identifying those unwholesome self-judgments that you know have been plaguing you, using the following mindfulness journal exercise.

Transform Your Unwholesome Self-Judgments

In your mindfulness journal, list what you've always thought of as your negative qualities. Include any criticisms others have made of you that you've been holding onto, whether it's something your siblings and peers used to say about you when you were a child, or what your boss told you in your last annual review. Don't stop to judge whether these judgments are accurate; that step comes next. Simply note what you think of as your flaws.

As your discomfort naturally arises, remain present with it. Recognize that it will soon pass away but for now is a valuable tool for helping you in the process of letting go of your unwholesome self-judgments. Let every painful belief about yourself arise, taking your time to become quiet and mindful, opening yourself up to this flow of awareness from your unconscious mind.

After you've written down all the harsh self-criticisms that have come to you, you may want to group them visually, drawing lines and circles to show connections to their origins, such as when your mother told you, "You move too slowly" or your spouse told you, "You procrastinate all the time." Find the common themes and note them.

Next, ask yourself the following questions about each of these unwholesome self-judgments:

1. *Is this true and accurate for me right now?*

2. *Is it true sometimes? Under what circumstances?*

3. *Was it true in the past, but no longer?*

If your self-judgment is not true and accurate for you right now, then envision yourself dragging these old beliefs and unwholesome patterns of thought into the trash, as if you were cleaning up your computer's virtual desktop, removing files that are no longer relevant or useful. Be forewarned that even if you make this choice to delete any particular self-judgment, it will probably continue to linger in your unconscious mind, arising again and again, particularly when you slow down and meditate. However, now you'll see it for what it is: an unwholesome, unproductive thought that causes pain and suffering. Be mindful of whenever it reemerges, and set it aside without further examination.

If your self-judgment is true, recognize it as an issue you'll be working with for some time. You can consciously change your tendency to cast that quality in an unwholesome light. Begin to write about ways in which this quality has benefited you or might benefit you in the future. You may even want to use a thesaurus to find words that mean the same thing, because it might shed some light on the various qualities of your self-judgment.

Next, write out an affirmation of the positive aspect of this self-judgment and recite it to yourself several times, while visualizing the positive feeling within your body (this is called an embodiment *of the quality), allowing yourself to feel the truth of the statement. For example:*

Unwholesome Self-Judgment	Wholesome Aspect	Affirmation/ Positive Embodiment
Disorganized	Creative, not contained by rigid structures	"I embrace my creativity and fluidity."
Sarcastic, cruel	Willing to defend myself and tell it like it is, honest, clever with words	"I am clever, forthright, and strong."
Unworthy	Worthiness, deserving, actualized	"I am worthwhile, I have substance, and I feel full and solid within."
Self-critical	Admiration and confirmation	"I fill myself up with compassion and acceptance, and I affirm myself."
Desire	I have passion and fire	"I am satisfied with contentment and equanimity."
Envy	I expect more of myself	"I admire others and appreciate everybody's uniqueness, and I aspire to greatness."
Sad	I am wide open with deep feelings	"My sadness breaks my heart open to feel compassion and grief."

Allow yourself to experience pride, delight, and comfort as you acknowledge the wholesome aspects of your self-judgment.

As you perform this exercise, you may feel that you're making excuses for yourself, but you're not. The paradox is that you can't acknowledge and drain the destructive power of your unwholesome self-judgments until you're less frightened by them. If you embrace your forthrightness and strength, and practice mindfulness, you'll notice when you're tempted to respond to someone with cruelty and sarcasm, and you'll instantly remember that you want to let go of that old behavior pattern. You'll begin to enhance the new neural network in your brain that fosters an awareness of your forthrightness and strength, and open up to your compassion and kindness. You'll stop feeling guilty and denying your tendency to be sarcastic, because you'll be compassionate toward yourself. Your compassion toward others will dissolve your desire to issue a cutting remark. Then, when your spouse or coworker makes a comment that you disagree with or that makes you uncomfortable, you'll be able to consciously choose a new, more wholesome and productive way of responding, changing the tenor of your relationship with them and fostering better relationships.

If your unwholesome self-judgments are particularly difficult to let go of, take heart in knowing that the approach of mindfulness-based cognitive therapy has been shown to be very effective with the most persistent unwholesome self-judgments that cause depressive thoughts and repeated relapses of clinical depression. In fact, this dual approach is more effective than most other psychotherapeutic approaches, including the use of antidepressant medication alone (Segal, Williams, and Teasdale 2002, 24–25). You don't have to allow old behavior patterns to sabotage your relationships with others or cause you to avoid addressing problems in a situation, setting yourself up for crisis.

Mulching Your Unwholesome Self-Judgments

Mulching has become something of a lost art. A good gardener knows that organic waste material can be placed in a mulch pile, where bacteria will break it down and turn it into fertilizer for growing something new. You can do the same with your unwholesome self-judgments, transforming them into the nutrients that will nourish your new self.

You transform your self-judgments by learning from them and discovering what they have to offer you. Whether it's an old unwholesome self-judgment that pops up here and there even though you've consciously rejected it, or one that you've only recently become aware of that's true and accurate today, the process is the same. Rather than ignore the moldy raspberries in the refrigerator or the dying leaves on your rosebush, you remove them and use them for mulch to enrich your life and allow you to grow something new. Like the painter or songwriter who mines the pain of her past to create a masterful work of art, or the former drug user who uses what he knows about addiction to help others address their own drug use, you may end up reinventing your life. Then again, you may simply discover that examining your thoughts and feelings about yourself yields insights into what you most want in your life, and how you might go about achieving it. Mulching allows you to turn any crisis into an opportunity and to use your unwholesome feelings and thoughts as fodder for personal exploration.

A client of mine, Alan, was embarrassed at a party after the conversation turned to a subject he felt he couldn't speak to, because he didn't have the education that the other party guests had. He explored with me his unwholesome self-judgment that was causing his pain that evening: "I'm unsophisticated." We talked about how he defined "unsophisticated" and whether or not it truly mattered to him if he couldn't easily contribute to the kinds of conversations he'd often felt left out of when talking to more-educated people. He rejected the idea that to be educated is to have certain tastes and interests, but said he still *felt* "unsophisticated."

I asked him, "Are you curious about whether there's any upside to being 'unsophisticated'?" Examining that idea, Alan decided that being "unsophisticated" had allowed him to focus on developing knowledge in areas he felt were more important than the topics his friends discussed. It allowed him to experience what Buddhists call "beginner's mind," a state of openness to learning that allows us to connect to our core self and its resources instead of closing down our creativity and believing we've learned all that we really need to learn.

Alan also realized that he did want to know more about one of the subjects a guest had raised, but had been feeling overextended and unable to devote time to educating himself in that area. He felt his guilt and frustration, and then let it go. He acknowledged that it wasn't an important enough topic to justify his view of himself as "unsophisticated" or inferior for not knowing more about it, and made a conscious decision to devote a specific block of time to taking a short course on the subject. The feeling of inadequacy that underlay this unwholesome self-judgment was part of his big story, the overarching narrative that he unknowingly created in childhood when he struggled in school and was told by his parents and teachers that he wasn't "college material." He recognized that the feeling and self-judgment was simply detritus churned up by his mind.

After consciously deciding that he really didn't care about "sophistication," Alan struggled with letting go of the old belief and putting into place a new view of himself. Over time, he was able to use mind-strength to install in his mind this new view and to overwrite "I'm unsophisticated" whenever it came into his awareness. In this way, his self-judgment actually supported his self-development the way nutrients in soil enhance a plant's growth. He broke down the self-judgment, extricated and used what was of value, and then discarded the rest.

When you mulch your self-criticisms, you bring yourself into balance as you acknowledge the wholesome aspects of a quality as well as its unwholesome aspects, instead of being drawn into the distorted belief that this quality exists inside you only in its unwholesome aspect. You discover the value in that quality and use it as nourishment while you let go of your negative judgment of it. For example, by discarding a label like "helicopter parent," and validating your close monitoring and careful guidance of your child, you help her move past the boundaries of her comfort zone and possibly discover that she has strength and coping abilities that neither you nor she had recognized. You acknowledge the unwholesome aspect of "hovering" and consciously choose to cease that behavior whenever you notice it, because you recognize that it doesn't serve you or your child. This discernment process allows you to transform an unwholesome self-judgment into a useful observation of how you operate, an insight that will help you embrace change.

In a crisis, it's difficult enough to tolerate the pain of loss without adding in the pain of acknowledging your qualities that sometimes manifest in an unwholesome way. With mindstrength, you'll be able to handle this extra layer of suffering. If you trust in the art of creative transformation, you'll feel reassured that this layer will dissipate very soon as a result of your engaging in this mulching process. You'll recognize that you're fertilizing and enriching the soil beneath you, allowing yourself to grow a new garden of self. You'll develop the strength to withstand even the most devastating crisis, because you'll know that in time, you'll bring forth something new that's organic and rich.

THE COURAGE TO UNCOVER YOUR UNWHOLESOME SELF-JUDGMENTS

In therapy, I can work with a client to examine the smallest of decisions that people tend to overlook in the course of a day. Cultivate mindfulness, and the witnessing self will arise unexpectedly as you go about your activities, alerting you to your entire mind-body awareness, including your discomfort. You may experience mindfulness as a flashlight that spotlights awareness of your conscience, or as a little voice whispering to you. When you're engaged in an angry confrontation, you might suddenly realize, "I don't like this; it's not good for me or the other person, and I need to stop." As you talk to your friend about her recent success, you'll notice as your envy mounts, and you'll think, "I'm really uncomfortable with what she's telling me. I need to explore the reason."

You may choose to take the time out to examine your self-judgments immediately, or you may come back to them later, when you're alone or with someone on your wisdom council of support.

WISDOM COUNCIL OF SUPPORT

Ask for help from a therapist, mentor, or wise partner from your wisdom council of support, someone who can help you to honestly examine your unwholesome self-judgments.

The following mindfulness journal exercise is one you can also engage in mentally any time you notice that you're engaging in self-criticism. Until you develop greater mindstrength, you'll likely silence the witnessing mind that calls attention to your discomfort, and need to explore the incident later, in detail, to discover what unwholesome self-judgments are causing your suffering. As you continue your mindfulness practice, however, you'll be able to stop in the moment and quickly go through these five steps, easing your discomfort and letting go of the unwholesome self-judgments that are part of your big story.

Discard an Unwholesome Self-Judgment

These are the steps to discarding an unwholesome self-judgment that you know is of no use to you and that causes you anguish. Use your mindfulness journal to work through each step:

1. Identity and label the judgment. *Give it a simple name or theme, such as "inadequate provider," "insincere," or "people pleaser."*

2. Discover the quality of the judgment. *Ask yourself, "What is this self-judgment causing me to think or feel about myself in this moment?" Does it make you feel ashamed, angry, or guilty, for example? Notice whether the feeling is wholesome and supportive of your well-being, or unwholesome, making it difficult for you to enter a state of spaciousness, openness, and trust.*

3. Find a remedy for the unwholesome thought or feeling. *Ask yourself, "Would I like to think or feel something different? What thought or feeling could I generate to shift myself out of this unwholesome state?"*

4. Formulate a new thought, image, or feeling, and begin to hold on to it firmly. *Experience it in your mind's eye and in your body. Feel a wholesome sensation, such as relaxation, excitement, or expansiveness.*

5. Assess whether you've shifted. *Ask yourself, "Have I shifted out of the feeling, state, or thought that was unwholesome and let go of my negative self-judgment?" If you have, then enjoy the new sensations, feelings, and thoughts you've generated as a remedy. If not, go back and repeat steps 1 through 4.*

The following Fertile Ground meditation uses guided imagery to help you mulch your self-judgments. It's a good idea to use this in conjunction with the previous mindfulness journal exercise, because it supports your conscious decision to stop engaging in self-criticism, and actually reprograms the brain by creating a new, more wholesome experience—albeit one that's happening in your mind.

Fertile Ground Meditation

As you sit, breathing in and out with long, slow breaths, focus your attention on your mind's eye, the space between your eyebrows that's also known as the "third eye" or "spiritual center." Bring mindful awareness to each and every negative, self-judgmental thought that arises, and watch for a theme to reveal itself (such as "bad person," "insincere," "inadequate," and so on).

Notice whether an unpleasant or uncomfortable feeling or sensation accompanies these unwholesome self-judgments. In your mind's eye, surround your self-judgment with a powerful beam of white light (or, if it's a sensation, imagine the white light surrounding the area in your body where you're experiencing it). Focus your mind, controlling this white light as if it were a powerful laser beam. Move the beam and the thought, feeling, or sensation enclosed within its circle of light away from your body and mind and into the earth. Watch as it sinks into the soil, intermingling with the rich, brown earth, which infuses it with nutrients as your laser beam turns into the diffuse, golden light of the sun, expanding outward, enveloping you, and warming the earth.

Bask in this sunlight as you feel roots beginning to extend downward from your feet, reaching into the nourishing earth and stretching outward. Then, drink in the healthy nutrients in that soil, pulling them up through your roots. Enjoy the feeling of strength that you create as you draw in power and nourishment.

WHOLESOME MEMORIES AS ANTIDOTES

Memories can be greatly distorted by strong, painful emotions that caused you to create unwholesome, distorted self-judgments. Returning to the original trauma from the safety of the present, particularly with a supportive therapist at your side, can allow you to look again at how events unfolded, using your logical mind to make sense of what you see with your mind's eye. When immersed in the original experience, you probably overlooked evidence that contradicted your emotional reality. As I mentioned before, when the children in my first-grade class laughed at my slurred speech that awful day when I was forced to speak in front of them, my emotional reality was that *everyone* laughed and *no one* showed support. In reality, such extremes are unlikely. In returning to such a memory, you might remember that one child shushed the others or that the teacher scolded those who were laughing. As you recall this evidence that the incident wasn't entirely negative, you can draw strength from the memory of someone's stepping in or your finding unexpected strength. Rather than allow a painful past experience to keep you in a state of contraction, you can remember its positive aspects and use them to give you courage.

The mind has the marvelous capacity to experience emotions connected to a prior memory over and over again, each time you recall that memory. When you close your eyes and imagine yourself standing at the shore of a lake, happily tossing in stones with your grandfather at your side, you recreate the feelings of contentment and love. You can use such a wholesome memory as an antidote to emotional pain whenever you feel unloved or insecure.

When a client has an unwholesome self-judgment, I help her experience its wholesome antidote. For example, an interior designer I work with felt that she wasn't unique or special. I knew from our sessions that this belief was holding her back from expanding her business in a creative way, which she needed to do in order to meet the goals she'd set for herself. I asked her to recall a time when she felt unique or special.

Sometimes my clients insist that they never, not for a moment, felt a particular wholesome quality, but I always press this point, because I know that with some effort, they can find one, however small. I tell the client that it's as if his computer has given him the error message "file not found" because he's searched for it in the wrong area of his hard drive. Through mindfulness meditation, we can recover such moments that the conscious mind has forgotten and "restore the file." Once you find and restore that file, you can reprogram your belief system, consciously choosing to lay a new neural network. However, if you decide to retain that file, you reinforce the old unwholesome belief, ensuring that it will affect your self-image in the future and limiting your opportunities for creative transformation that would lead to deeper fulfillment.

You can return repeatedly to this wholesome memory, all the while using it as a positive antidote. When you do, you'll reinforce a new, consciously chosen, wholesome self-judgment. My client was able to access a memory of putting her senior art project on display for the class, and the tremendous admiration and respect her classmates showered on her. Each time she recalled this memory, it re-created in her feelings of being talented, creative, and special.

CREATING A NEW MEMORY

Another technique for transforming an unwholesome self-judgment into a wholesome one is to consciously rewrite a traumatic memory. Doing so lessens the intensity of the unwholesome feelings attached to it and lays new neural networks for remembering a positive, enhancing experience (albeit one created in the imagination). By creating this healing memory, you ensure that whenever the original memory arises in your awareness, it won't cause you as much pain as it used to.

A Memory Made Wholesome

After meditating for several minutes, turn your mind's eye to the scene of an upsetting memory, recalling exactly where you were, how you felt, and any sensory experiences you had at the time (remembering the sensory aspects will help you remove any unwholesome feelings that come up when you have similar experiences in the future, for instance, if you usually become agitated when it rains, because you associate it with that unpleasant memory). Put yourself completely in the scene.

As the scene starts to unfold, imagine yourself being drawn upward and backward by an invisible source that deposits you in a balcony seat from which you gaze down at the drama before you. Be aware that you're writing the script of this play, and begin to rewrite it. Imagine that in the moment of your embarrassment, the people around you express support, smiling and encouraging you to continue.

Experience the discomfort of this moment mingling with your rising courage, and allow yourself to breathe deeply. Move the feelings through your body as you rewrite the scene to unfold in a way that alleviates your discomfort and makes you feel reassured of being loved and accepted by the people around you.

LETTING GO OF THE FALSE SELF AND "BECOMING NOBODY"

The false self, also called the "ego" or the "egoic mind," is the self we identify with when we're focused on our own needs or importance. The false self is not "bad," but identifying solely with this self, rather than the core self, leads to unwholesome thoughts, feelings, and behaviors. The more we engage in egoic mind, the harder it is to handle a crisis. The ego must move out of the way if we're to immerse ourselves in the three-step process of creative transformation. In the state of open mind, the ego's voice is but a whisper, drowned out by the call of our soul.

The false self is overly influenced by external voices that we internalize, voices that say "You aren't good enough unless you..." or "You'll suffer unless you..." Fear dominates the thinking of the false self and causes us to become self-absorbed, defensive, or overly identified with our roles and situations. When change comes, the false self is alarmed and urges us to resist in an attempt to avoid suffering.

To prevent the false self from taking charge, spiritual teacher Ram Dass suggests the dramatic step of an advanced practice he calls "going into nobody training" (Dass 2007). "Becoming nobody" means letting go of your preconceived notions about your roles and practicing open mind, allowing yourself to discover what's beyond those roles that the false self fiercely clings to, because even the most positive role can limit us and hold us back.

Raised in a prominent Boston family, Richard Alpert knew very early in his childhood that his family expected him to follow in his father's and grandfather's footprints. He went on to become a psychologist and professor at Berkeley and Harvard in the 1960s, but was fired after his experiments with LSD at Harvard. It was a devastating blow, because he was completely identified with being a well-respected psychologist, author, and professor. However, because of LSD, he had experienced open-mind consciousness, so he was ultimately able to break away from this overidentification with the roles he'd played as a psychologist and professor, and let go of his parents' expectations, which had caused him to walk this particular path. Only then was he able to forge a new life as a spiritual teacher, and develop a new identity as Ram Dass. He came to realize that despite all the trappings of success, including having his own private plane and the admiration of his students, his former life had made him profoundly unhappy, an uncomfortable truth he'd avoided facing for years. The crisis of loss made him realize that though the mandala he'd created may have seemed wholesome and good, it didn't represent the calling of his soul. "Becoming nobody," silencing his false self, allowed him to access his core self and form a new, far more fulfilling mandala for himself.

Inside all of us lie possibilities that might sound preposterous to us in the present moment. To access them, we must undergo the art of creative transformation. Next, you'll learn about letting go of something as unwholesome, unproductive, and even destructive as negative self-judgments: the need to be in control.

CHAPTER 7

Let Go of the Need to Be in Control

Do not pursue the past.
Do not lose yourself in the future.
The past no longer is.
The future is yet to come.
Look deeply at life as it is
in the very here and now,
dwelling in stability and freedom.

—Buddha

A few years ago, I was brought into a record company to help resolve a crisis that was plaguing the marketing team. I asked to sit in on their strategy meeting and, within minutes, noticed that while all of these creative people had the same goal, they were all fighting for control of the situation. Each tried to pressure the others to back off from their positions and come around to their own. All were driven by the same fear: that their current number-one recording artist's latest CD wasn't selling as well as expected. Panic had set in, and the shouting and accusations had begun.

Very quickly, I interrupted to ask if I might lead them in a ten-minute mindfulness meditation before they continued the discussion.

Although their faces told me they thought this was a colossal waste of time when they had important business to conduct, they had hired me to help, and decided they'd better make at least some attempt at following my directions. The room was restless at first, but soon, everyone was in a mindful state, completely quiet.

I instructed them to open their eyes and wait for a moment. Then I said, "Let's go around the room, and I want each of you to tell me what you experienced while meditating." As they shared what images and thoughts had come up for them, they started to recognize that they all experienced similar fears and concerns. They realized that they all saw the core problem and wanted to solve it, whereas before, all they had perceived was a power struggle—one each had been determined to win.

It took only ninety minutes for everyone to find common ground and get to the heart of what had worked for this recording artist in the past and why the formula had been put aside. Some of the executives admitted that they were afraid the artist would be offended if they asked her to do a core piece of publicity she'd done before she became a star. They'd assumed she couldn't be convinced to "lower herself" to push the album in this tried-and-true way. Open at last to the possibility that the old solution might be the right one in this situation, they agreed to approach her. The star readily agreed to their plan, and soon after the new marketing push, the recording shot to the top of the charts.

Whenever we're facing an unpleasant or alarming situation, we're likely to become anxious and try to figure out what we can do instead of becoming quiet and seeking new ideas or revisiting what worked in the past. We quickly make a decision about our course and focus on getting others to agree to go along with the program. This desire to take control can lead to great suffering.

BUDDHISM'S FOUR NOBLE TRUTHS— AND CONTROL ISSUES

Twenty-five hundred years ago, the Buddha offered insights into how we cause ourselves mental anguish and how we can free ourselves from the patterns of thinking and behaving that perpetuate our suffering. In a sense, the Buddha was the very first psychologist, teaching people about the power of changing their mental processes in order to alleviate emotional discomfort and embrace change.

By looking at the central tenets of Buddhism, the four noble truths and the eightfold path, we can better understand why we become agitated and respond by trying to micromanage our circumstances. These truths teach us how we can let go of our attachments so that we can transform our lives in an innovative way. Controlling behavior, as you'll see, may provide a temporary illusion of power and safety, because in the moment, it may seem that it's working for you, but this type of approach always leads to increased suffering for everyone. Fortunately, the four noble truths will help you see how to break out of the need to be in control and, instead, enter into an acceptance of the present moment. Only in the present will you find the courage to enter the unknown and relax into the changes you cannot avoid.

The four noble truths are as follows:

The first noble truth: In life, there is suffering, because of the impermanent nature of things. (This is the problem.)

The second noble truth: Suffering is due to attachments and expectations, to grasping and clinging. (This is the nature of the problem.)

The third noble truth: It's possible to end suffering by giving up attachments (clinging) and expectations (grasping). (This is the promise.)

The fourth noble truth: The way to end suffering due to clinging and grasping is the middle way of the eightfold path. (This is the solution.)

Let's look at each of these truths in detail and see how they can free you from the need to be in control, allowing you to let go of this form of resistance and move forward out of your dilemma.

THE FIRST NOBLE TRUTH: IN LIFE, THERE IS SUFFERING, BECAUSE OF THE IMPERMANENT NATURE OF THINGS.

Because we feel more secure when we have a sense of predictability, we develop a great capacity for denying a simple truth: that nothing stays the same. Cities are wiped out by natural disasters; perfectly healthy people suddenly die; the consequences of our actions come into being; and we're forced to admit that even if we do everything "right" and exercise every precaution, we can still face unexpected loss.

When your illusions are dispelled by a crisis you thought could never happen, you recognize how illogical your denial was, and may begin to feel foolish or ashamed, or guilty that you didn't prepare for change. The thought of what other ugly surprises may be in store can be frightening. Unwholesome feelings such as these make it even harder to regain equanimity and exercise nonreactivity, but both are crucial if you're to influence your situation positively.

Too often, rather than surrender to the inevitability of change and work creatively with it, people resort to the fear-based behavior of trying to take charge and force other people and situations to conform to their expectations. The first noble truth of Buddhism is a reminder not to slip into the avoidance behavior of denial. While it's not wise to create gloomy thoughts about how matters might take a turn for the worse, consciously ignoring the reality that all situations transform sets you up for a great shock when that time comes. With mindfulness, you can remain aware of, for example, the harsh reality that your health has taken a turn for the worse and your current way of working with it is becoming obsolete, yet not be paralyzed or obsessed by this knowledge. You can accept that you must alter your eating habits and let go of the desire to take control of the situation in a vain attempt to avoid this change. Similarly, by remembering the first noble truth, you can learn to tolerate being in a relationship with someone you love who's unsure of whether or not to remain with you and needs time to sort out his or her feelings.

THE SECOND NOBLE TRUTH: SUFFERING IS DUE TO ATTACHMENTS AND EXPECTATIONS, TO GRASPING AND CLINGING.

Your inability to avoid change may make you angry, sad, and frustrated. It can be hard to let go of the false belief that the only way to achieve happiness again is to regain what's been lost. Even when you know you can't reverse the situation, you may agonize over this reality. The strong desire to return to the past, which we all tend to idealize, can cause you to try to force situations to revert to their previous state. You might grudgingly accept that the tide has turned while you keep holding on to inner, hidden resistance that your conscious mind denies.

Clinging to what once was, avoiding the process of grief and acceptance, causes paralysis. Grasping for a future set of circumstances identical to the past holds you back from discovering what better roads lie ahead, outside of your sight. The desire to backtrack or reconstruct will likely result in your walking around in circles, lost in the dark woods, instead of peering around corners to find new paths.

THE THIRD NOBLE TRUTH: IT'S POSSIBLE TO END SUFFERING BY GIVING UP ATTACHMENTS (CLINGING) AND EXPECTATIONS (GRASPING). The shift in perspective that comes when we recognize that there's no such thing as a permanent sense of happiness begins our healing from suffering. The next step is to accept that we must broaden our definition of what we need in order to be happy, giving up the habits of clinging and grasping, as well as the need to control external circumstances.

Most of us tend to place many restrictions on our happiness, insisting that unless we have *x*, *y*, and *z*, we can't possibly find joy. We may say that we can be contented as long as we can lead the good life. But when we admit that it's been five years since the end of our last long-term relationship, that our bills are going up while our income remains the same, and that we've begun to develop aches and pains and chronic health issues that never seem to go away, discontent begins to rumble within us. We start clinging and grasping, and struggling to fix our problems so that we can return to our former state of happiness.

After emerging from the shock of a great loss, we're even more despairing about the possibility of being joyful again. However, the third noble truth offers us the promise of a new way of living that's as satisfying, if not more fulfilling, than the old. It beckons us to begin the process of transformation.

THE FOURTH NOBLE TRUTH: THE WAY TO END SUFFERING DUE TO CLINGING AND GRASPING IS THE MIDDLE WAY OF THE EIGHTFOLD PATH. It's important to balance a thirst for something better with an acceptance of what is, right now. Balance allows you to live in the present moment and trust that your acceptance will clear the mist of confusion and distractions, and show you the way to move forward into happiness again. Here's the paradox of change: until you can accept what is, you cannot move into what might be.

The Buddha said that all of life's conflicts include the following:

- ❧ Letting go or holding on

- ❧ Opening to the present or clinging to the past

- ❧ Expanding or contracting

Similarly, Dr. Frederick Perls, the founder of gestalt therapy, often said that when we cling to the past or what no longer serves us, we contract ourselves to the point where we're unable to be nourished and invigorated by the present moment (Simkin 1976). We have to accept that what's past has truly passed in order to open up to what the present moment offers us.

All of the steps along the eightfold path bring us out of despair and pain, and into the light of hope and possibility, out of the past and into the present, where we can see the way to a better future.

THE EIGHTFOLD PATH

The eightfold path outlined by the Buddha will help you understand how you can accept the impermanent nature of things, stop clinging and grasping, and let go of the need to control the situations you find yourself in. They are the keys to finding a balance between acceptance and doing what needs to be done to positively affect your circumstances.

The Eightfold Path	
1. Wise view	These two form the basis of wisdom.
2. Wise intention	
3. Wise speech	These three form the basis of ethical conduct.
4. Wise action	
5. Wise livelihood	

6. Wise effort	These three form the basis of proper mental development and mindstrength.
7. Wise mindfulness	
8. Wise concentration	

Wise View

As long as you hold on to the view that you can take charge of the situation and force it to become tolerable again, you do not hold wise view.

In wise view, you recognize that it's not your job, nor is it in your power, to control what happens outside of you. You understand that instead, you must control what happens within your own mind. Then, and only then, can you stop operating out of anxiety, fear, insecurity, and distrust, and instead allow wholesome emotions to guide your thoughts and behaviors.

Clients have told me that they were in the situation where a partner's behavior was intolerably cruel or manipulative, yet I knew that if they were to make the obvious choice to leave, it was likely they would soon find themselves in an equally difficult situation because of their unresolved issues. If a client is married to someone who isn't physically abusive or intimidating but is very verbally disrespectful and belittling, I'll help her find ways to cope with the situation while she builds mindstrength and accesses her core creativity so that she can begin forming a plan for how to leave the relationship. The anxious desire to fix the other person begins to fade as mindstrength builds and hope for a better situation begins to appear over the horizon.

Wise Intention

In Buddhism, we say it's wrong to control, dominate, or manipulate others, because that would harm them and prevent us from knowing what it's like to experience a loss of control. Not knowing what's coming next is crucial for surrendering to the possibilities hidden in the unknown.

To exercise wise intention, you must be mindful of any propensity toward allowing your fear to rule you. When operating from a primitive, fearful state, everything seems to be a threat to survival, and the mind begins to justify actions it otherwise would recognize as domineering and manipulative. I've heard many eloquent excuses for being dishonest with a loved one, violating a confidence, and secretly sabotaging another person. Fear can blind us, and our intention can become selfish, because we seek to build our sense of power and security no matter what the cost.

From both a Buddhist and a psychological view, if you have an unwholesome intention and are consciously choosing to manipulate others, you're limiting your own capacity for change and stunting the creative unfolding of your own life. Your energy is being wasted on the futile effort of trying to force the external world to conform to your vision. The mental and emotional effort required to maintain a pretense of integrity when you're secretly lying or cheating is enormous. Having wise intention is more than merely ethical; it's necessary for psychological well-being and clear thinking.

Mindfulness boosts your awareness. Instead of being completely immersed in an experience that you're unwittingly manipulating, you'll experience a sense, however fleeting, that you're doing something unwholesome. An uncomfortable thought such as, "I'm trying to make him feel guilty so that he does what I want him to," or "I ought to let her know that I disagree, but it's easier for me to say yes and work behind her back to do what I really want" may arise. Instead of quickly dismissing it, you'll allow yourself to experience any guilt or shame that arises. Then you'll consciously and bravely explore why you feel the need to resort to manipulation and control. This discovery process will give you the strength to accept the situation exactly as it is, even if you don't like it, and use positive means to influence it for the better.

Wise intention leads to wise action, problem solving, solution seeking, and wholesome interaction. It helps you trust that you'll be able to work with others to create a situation that benefits everyone involved instead of assuming that you have to hide your motivations and try to direct the situation from the wings.

Traditionally, Buddhists say that wise view and wise intention are the foundations of wisdom. Wisdom starts with wise view, and is deepened by your awareness of your motivations and how wrong intent causes you suffering instead of letting you move forward into positive change.

Wise Speech

The greater our facility with language, the more tempting it can be to try to control situations through our words. Insults and sarcasm can intimidate others, and someone who's very verbally gifted may use these techniques to manipulate others in a subtle or not-so-subtle way. This behavior is particularly common when someone's in a crisis and feels threatened. Gossip unfairly gives us power over others. Left-handed compliments designed to make someone doubt himself and feel weak, or carefully constructed insults designed to humiliate another person while preventing him from recognizing that he's being ridiculed publicly, are common weapons in the arsenal of one who doesn't exercise wise speech.

Wise speech, a wholesome response to changes that are out of your control, requires mindful attention to the power of your words and the messages underneath them. Recognize that your tone of voice, facial expression, and body language matter, and drop any defensiveness that arises in you when someone points out the discrepancy between the literal meaning of your words and the message you're sending with your eyes, crossed arms, or disrespectful tone.

Wise speech has nothing to do with how cleverly we can use words to hurt or intimidate others and establish our power. It requires speaking with honesty and respect for the listener and ourselves, and trusting that a wholesome interaction will lead to a positive outcome.

Direct, honest communication can be very uncomfortable and even painful, especially if you're not used to engaging in it, but wise speech is vital if you want to have more productive, more respectful conversations. Often, I've counseled managers who had no idea just how intimidating or disrespectful they were when speaking to employees. When in a panic, they tended to respond with aggressive speech meant to frighten others into changing their behavior in order to placate the boss. This approach shuts down productive communication, reducing the manager's ability to see the larger picture, make better decisions, and effectively influence her team. Good leaders carefully hone what they say, mindfully expressing themselves.

When we cultivate wise speech, we don't fear saying something wrong. However, we're more attuned to the quality of our words and their effect on others. We speak up and say, "You seem upset by what I just said. Have I hurt your feelings?" inviting the other person to let go of his suffering. Wise speech fosters good relationships and partnerships and prevents future crises.

Sometimes, we should speak up in order to influence someone to change, but wise speech requires that we do so kindly and respectfully. Although it may seem well meaning, being blunt or tactless with another is unkind and usually motivated not by a genuine desire to help that person but by the need to feel superior and be intimidating. Wise speech is gentle, never cruel or harsh. It enhances the situation by inviting everyone to improve it instead of shutting down the communication process.

To speak the truth respectfully, you must let go of your desire to pressure others into doing what you want. At some point, you may discern that no matter how often you say the same thing with kindness, honesty, and compassion, you'll never affect the other person the way you'd like. Part of wise speech is letting go of your attachment to having your words change the way others think, feel, or behave.

Wise Action

Wise action means not acting in controlling, manipulative, or coercive ways. It means not being vengeful, regardless of how badly you've been hurt. The thirst for revenge comes from clinging to the past and to the lost opportunity to prevent suffering. People can obsess over what they should've done differently, and sometimes that obsession turns into vengefulness as they try to "right" a wrong.

By mindfully accepting that the past can never be re-created, that the moment came and went, you can return your focus to the present and the future. You can start to imagine what might be instead of constantly turning over in your mind what was. The need to make others see that they were wrong or admit that they caused you harm dissipates as you use mindstrength to turn your attention back to the present moment and what you can do, right now, to create a better situation.

Wise action means being honest in all of your dealings rather than making excuses for cheating others. The desire to take what isn't rightfully yours is rooted in a fear that you can't be happy unless you have more: more money, more power, or more influence. If you're mindful, you can discover the unwholesome beliefs that drive your dishonest actions and begin to deconstruct them.

Wise action also means doing the right thing even when it's uncomfortable to do so. A great leader is willing to stand up and blow the whistle, declaring, "This isn't acceptable," regardless of whether it makes anyone angry. The desire to control others' emotions and avoid their disapproval is often what's behind our unwillingness to engage in wise action. Once we've taken that bold step into doing what's right, we can begin our creative transformation instead of resisting change out of the fear that people won't like us. Mindstrength enables us to tolerate differences between our own and others' views, and forge ahead with confidence that we're doing what's right for us and for others.

Wise Livelihood

Livelihood refers not just to what you do for a living but your purpose, which weaves meaning into every action. You may play many roles in your life that have meaning for you: parent, community organizer, retail-store manager, caretaker, educator, healer, and so on. Whatever your livelihood, whatever you spend your time doing, whatever it is that gives you a sense of purpose, Buddhist tradition says that you must do it mindfully, giving it the focus and effort it deserves, and being open to new possibilities for deepening your ability to use your talents for the betterment of all. *Dharma*, the "way" or "path," is the Buddhist term for our responsibility to help others. We live out our dharma when we make the most of our opportunities and gifts, using them as tools to improve and enhance our world. This creates a sense of purpose and joy, and gives us the strength to resist the temptation to panic and try to force the world to meet our expectations.

A teacher who exercises wise livelihood doesn't resist learning about a new way of teaching or about a pupil's unfamiliar learning disability. The teacher doesn't insist that her years of teaching excuse her from the need to develop new skills. Instead, she's open to learning something new or trying a novel way of presenting material that will work for such children. She's willing to embrace change and the unknown.

Wise livelihood puts us in touch with our most creative self. As a therapist, I see myself primarily practicing as an artist. Every day, I look with fresh eyes to see what new colors and textures I might use to assist my clients in opening up to the present moment and discovering what it offers.

Most people in the world are just trying to put food on the table and a roof over their heads, and may never have the opportunity to turn passion into livelihood. However, anyone can practice wise livelihood in their interactions with others and, in doing so, let go of the need to control others or manipulate situations in order to gain power.

Sometimes when I'm in a New York City cab, the driver won't say a word for the entire ride. He may take the most efficient route to my destination, or may hope that I'm distracted and won't notice that he's made a few extra turns to pad the fare a bit. I'm vigilant about this, because I know that people sometimes try to cheat "just a little" in the hopes of getting more money. Recently, a taxi driver engaged me in a long and fascinating conversation about families and immigrants. He talked about his father in Pakistan and asked me about mine in Boston. I was so involved in the conversation, as was he, that when we were a few blocks from my hotel, he turned off the meter early—and I ended up tipping him more than he would've made if he'd left the meter on. This driver practices wise livelihood. He sees that his job can be more than simply transporting passengers from point A to point B, and recognizes that he'll be rewarded amply if he lets go of his worries about how much money he'll make and focuses instead on living out his purpose, or dharma.

People who are unhappy with their work often become controlling and rigid. They become bureaucrats who are more interested in exercising their power rather than practicing wise livelihood. Unable to approach their work creatively, they hold tightly to the present situation—job title, the way things have always been done, and the pecking order—and overlook the possibility of a creative transformation that would lead to greater happiness.

Wise speech, wise action, and wise livelihood are the three foundations of ethical conduct. When we exercise them, we readily dismiss unwholesome self-judgments that arise into our awareness. We don't trick others into doing things our way out of the fear that we'd suffer otherwise. We approach change without resistance and recognize what we must do in order to respect ourselves and others. We act and speak with honesty, and have a clear conscience.

Wise Effort

To exercise wise effort is to do the work of focusing and disciplining your mind to align it with your wise intention. It's very easy to resort to controlling behavior in a difficult situation, even if you intend not to, because of the well-established neural networks in your brain. Building mindstrength through mindfulness practice increases your ability to be optimistic and enthusiastic rather than pessimistic and depressive. It allows you to experience a sense of expansion and possibility rather than the contractedness and fear that lead to small thinking and to controlling behavior. Wise effort requires letting go of what no longer works and engaging in courageous new actions that lead to transformation.

Wise Mindfulness

Mindfulness is what grounds you in the present so that when you start to drift off into obsessing about the past, or start making plans to wrest control of a situation, you stop and look deeply at your negative and controlling patterns. Being fully focused on what's happening in the moment, experiencing your unwholesome and painful feelings, requires mindstrength. Your pain, grief, or anger doesn't have to overwhelm you and draw you into avoidance behaviors. Find a way to get support from others, relying on members of a wisdom council of support (see chapter 11) so that it's easier for you to remain on the eightfold path.

As you develop the habit of being present with your feelings, you'll notice an increasing sense of strength and self-control. You'll have greater confidence in your ability to manage your emotions and stay calm. You may even find wholesome emotions and thoughts unexpectedly arising in you as you experience wise mindfulness. Even a few minutes of mindfulness meditation can infuse you with a deep sense of comfort and free you of the desire to try to fix everyone and everything around you.

Wise Concentration

By exercising wise concentration, you remain present in your awareness of a situation exactly as it is, and instead of being reactive, you'll find that you suddenly know how to respond to it in a wholesome, productive way. You'll be able to focus on what's going on inside you instead of what's going on outside of you. A heightened focus, caused by wise concentration, will make you more intuitive as you pick up on subtleties you would otherwise overlook, subtleties that may be big clues about what your next step should be. You'll be able to tell that your partner isn't being honest with you, and instead of reacting with fear or anger, you can remain present with that feeling, explore it, and find the words to approach her and invite her to join you in an honest conversation.

Wise effort, wise mindfulness, and wise concentration form the basis of mental discipline. They give us the mindstrength to face the situation exactly as it is and let go of any desire to prove that we're in control of the wheel of fate. In fact, they allow us to recognize that we're never completely powerless, so there's no need to automatically resist the turn of the wheel and foster the illusion that we're the ones in charge of its movement. We always have the choice to change our lives from the inside out by exercising mental discipline and wisdom, and recognizing the power we have to end our suffering. We can always step forward into a better situation by practicing the art of creative transformation.

WHEN YOU CAN'T CONTROL SOMEONE ELSE'S DECISION

It can be extremely stressful to have to back off and give someone else room to make a serious decision, for example, a loved one who has to choose between two different medical treatments for a life-threatening illness; a romantic or business partner who's thinking about ending his relationship with you; or an elderly, increasingly fragile parent who's facing a potential move into a retirement community. The desire to figure out the "best" course of action (and to believe that there *is* a "best" course) and to convince the other person to take it flares up with intensity. You can issue an ultimatum to pressure someone into making a decision, in the hope that you can reduce your anxiety and propensity to obsess about the outcome, but sometimes deadlines come and go and the other person still has not made a decision.

When you're in limbo, you must first accept that you're not in control of the other person. The only thing you can control is your mind's process. You may feel less anxious and frustrated if you set up a plan for what to do if the person doesn't make the decision you hope for. However, when that moment comes, you may find yourself unable to follow through on your threat to leave the marriage, dissolve the company, or stop listening to your mother complain about how lonely she is. Mindstrength, accepting the four noble truths, and following the eightfold path will make it easier to remain in a state of flux and accept the outcome if it's not what you desired, and move forward in the way that's most wholesome for you. The practice of mindful awareness allows you to tolerate ambivalence, ambiguity, and conflict, as well as reduce frustration, ward off unwholesome thoughts and feelings, and resist the urge to force the situation.

Nonreactivity requires that you have mindstrength and compassion for both the other person and yourself. It's not easy to have no control over a decision that will powerfully affect your future, and let go of your desire to know what will unfold, but sometimes, doing nothing is the best course. Mindfulness practice will build your compassion and prevent you from retreating into panic, fear, and unwholesome thoughts and feelings.

I've found that my clients who are in this difficult situation benefit from answering the following questions, which is like taking the pulse of the here and now, and will build mindstrength and stop your reactivity:

1. What do I feel right now?

2. Do these feelings benefit me in any way? If I feel anxious and fearful, do these emotions lead me to insights, or are they completely unwholesome responses that cause conflict, hold me back, and distract and disempower me?

3. If what I'm experiencing is in response to another person's behavior, what's the evidence that that person's actions have little or nothing to do with me and are, instead, the result of what's going on inside his own mind?

4. Is there anything I can do to help myself depersonalize the situation?

5.   Are there practices I can use to nourish myself at this difficult time?

Of course, I strongly recommend being even more dedicated to mindfulness practice during times of transition, but I also recommend this visualization exercise, which will shift you out of a sense of powerlessness or urgency and allow you to be more comfortable in your uncertainty. It's very effective for helping you to trust the transformation process and dispel your fear of not being in control of a situation.

The Lone Explorer Meditation

After a few minutes of mindfulness meditation, begin to imagine that you are traveling with a group of explorers in the desert, riding camels toward a large oasis up ahead. As you reach the oasis, like everyone else, you dismount from your camel. The others immediately approach the central pool and begin washing up and quenching their thirst with handfuls of water. While your fellow explorers mingle by the pool, you become curious and contain your immediate desire to refresh yourself. You begin to follow a path through the palm trees, up a narrow path, and down the other side.

To your surprise and delight, you come across a beautiful, isolated pool. You marvel at the waterfalls cascading down the rock and emptying into this pool. You dip your hand in the clear water that has been cooled by the shade of the many palm trees surrounding it, and drink your fill of sparkling water.

At the far edge of the pool, you spot a carpet of lush green grass. You amble over to it and lie down, resting yourself and feeling your body rejuvenate. You're glad that your curiosity and patience has led you to a cooler, more wonderful pool than the first one. You feel nourished and relaxed, and you rest here, alone yet feeling nourished and deeply connected to your core self.

After a time, you notice that there's a cool, moist breeze blowing across your face and hair. You recognize that it's time to rejoin your party of explorers, so you arise and slowly walk back over the hill toward the main pool. As you descend the hill and rejoin the group, your mind is clear and focused.

When you're lying by the pool in your imagination, allow any images to arise. Note them and explore them after you've completed your meditation, perhaps writing about them in your mindfulness journal.

All of us have within us a reservoir of untapped creativity, but the pathway to it escapes our notice if we don't let go of our fears and resentments, and take our first steps into the mysterious forest, trusting that we'll find the footpath to something new and rewarding. If we can surrender to the process, we can move forth with enthusiasm and curiosity.

Whenever you've been taken advantage of or harmed in some way, it's only natural to be reactive and to feel angry and betrayed. Thoughts of revenge may begin to formulate in your mind like gathering storm clouds before you exercise wise effort, letting go of bad intent and working to regain your sense of equanimity.

Focusing on convincing others that what they did was wrong and that they should apologize and make amends usually leads to further suffering. If the person didn't have wise intention and either didn't care if you got hurt or actually wanted to hurt you, recognize that you probably have very little power to change people's attitudes and make them behave more compassionately toward you. Let go of that need to control the other person. If this person's behavior was rooted in carelessness, you're far more likely to influence the person when you exercise wise view, wise intention, wise speech, and wise effort. Remember, you can't control others, but you can control yourself, by controlling your thoughts. Once you've truly accepted this wise view, you'll feel both liberated from suffering and empowered to take charge of your life and move forward into creating a new mandala.

PART III

Tune In: Attaining Wise Mind, Open Mind

CHAPTER 8

Accessing Core Creativity and Awakening Open Mind

You lose your grip,
and then you slip
Into the masterpiece.

—Leonard Cohen, "A Thousand Kisses Deep"

Most of us were taught that creativity comes from the thoughts and emotions of the mind. The greatest singers, dancers, painters, writers, and filmmakers recognize that the most original, and even transformative, ideas actually come from the core of our being. Core creativity emerges when we're in a state of open-mind consciousness, which evolves from mindful inquiry.

In open mind, you experience a sense of spaciousness as your anxieties about time and your perceptions of limited options fall away, and you feel yourself open up to receive knowledge and ideas that were previously hidden from your awareness. It's as if the self who has been trying to figure out the next step has been completely overshadowed by the self that's connected to a force of creativity that stretches beyond the boundaries created by your mind. You feel expansive and, at times, exuberant, as if all obstacles have been dissolved, and you find the courage to make dramatic changes. Breakthroughs occur suddenly, as if a door not only appeared just a moment before, but swung wide open, allowing the light of awareness to stream through. All confusion lifts.

CONTACTING THE CORE

Meditating on any of these access states can bring you into open mind, where you can access the resources of your core creativity.

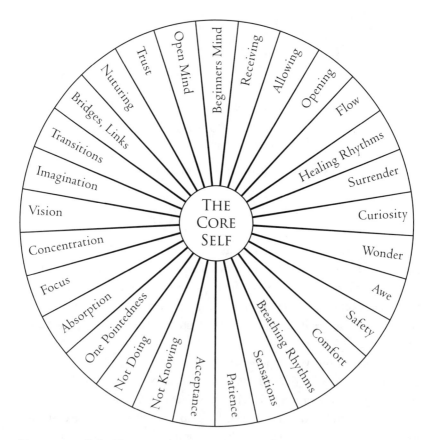

FIGURE 8.1 CONTACTING THE CORE

RESOURCES OF THE CORE

*Having accessed core creativity in open-mind consciousness,
you'll also discover other resources.*

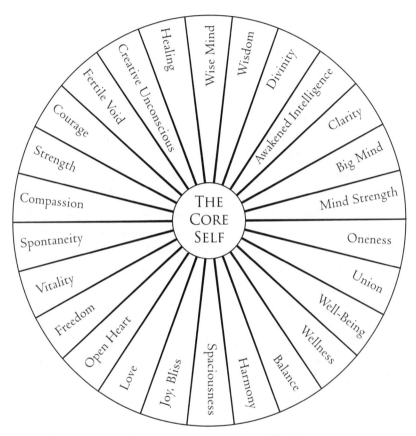

FIGURE 8.2 RESOURCES OF THE CORE

CORE CREATIVITY, OPEN MIND, AND
SPIRITUAL AWAKENING

Achieving open mind usually requires training the mind to quiet the
automatic chatter of the rational brain and invite the intuitive, dreaming

brain, the right hemisphere, to bring its wisdom into your awareness. In ancient traditions, open-mind consciousness was considered to be a spiritual awakening, the great enlightenment that dissolves the darkness of confusion and fear, and ushers in peace, happiness, clarity, and contentment. As you know by now, until you embrace the current moment completely, finding perfection even in the pain and chaos surrounding you, you can't move forward into a better future, one that's filled with possibilities. Instead, you'll be stuck struggling with wanting mind, perceiving obstacles everywhere, and holding yourself back and creating suffering.

The old notion that there's one formulaic way to achieve this spiritual awakening and creative vibrancy has been blown apart. You don't have to practice meditation for thirty years before attaining a breakthrough. A few years ago, I took on a client named Sarah, who'd completely given up on psychotherapy until a failed suicide attempt convinced her to try therapy one more time. I urged her to begin a mindfulness practice, and she agreed. After several months—not years, but months—she had an extremely powerful experience while meditating. As she described it, she felt a rush of light and energy infuse her body, and experienced an ineffable sense of the presence of the divine, the cosmos, and a collective consciousness. She said it was as if she were with an old, dear friend who was giving her a deep sense of comfort and trust. Had she known about this state of consciousness before attempting to take her life, she told me, she probably wouldn't have done so. After this transcendent experience, Sarah, who'd been overweight to an unhealthy degree, lost several pounds, became more engaged by her work and closer to her friends, and was no longer suicidal. It was a major turning point for her. (Rand & Alexander, 2007.)

What Sarah described has been called not only "open-mind awareness" but also, in the West, a "peak experience," "being in the flow," or "being in the zone." I call it the experience of "core creativity," because I believe that deep inside every person lies this potential for connecting to a universal flow of knowledge and creativity that's boundless and expansive. Our individual thoughts and memories are a part of this greater, larger resource.

Core creativity has tremendous transformative powers. It allows you to let go of all vestiges of resistance, fully accept that the old mandala has been swept away, and eagerly form a new one out of a sense of passion and purpose, rather than quickly assemble one from whatever's at hand. When you experience core creativity in a state of open-mind awareness, you feel as if you're fully alive yet also immersed in aliveness itself, enveloped by a numinous force that's intertwined with all of creation. You feel as if you've soared upward to an eagle's perch and are surveying all the wisdom and knowledge that's available to you, outside of you *and* within you.

Although it may feel as if you're channeling pure creativity from the gods or the muses, what's actually happening is that your mind is synthesizing this hidden knowledge and fashioning something new. Later, if you go back, you may be able to see that your own experiences influenced your bold and innovative idea. When you're in the experience of accessing your core creativity, however, you may find it hard to believe that you're actually in charge of this marvelous flow.

THE EXPERIENCE OF CORE CREATIVITY

Whether accessed through meditation or through toning your creativity overall (which you'll learn more about later in the chapter), core creativity is a remarkable catalyst for change because of its qualities of hopefulness, spaciousness, expansiveness, and limitlessness. In open mind, when your core creativity arises to the surface of your awareness, you feel blissful and ecstatic. The limitations of your perception dissolve. The observer and the observed seem to be united as a sense of time and the constriction of fear melt away.

Core creativity can lead to a breakthrough in parenting or relating to others, or it can make you feel vitalized and fully engaged in the mundane chores of the day. The Buddha said that to find enlightenment, one must chop wood and carry water, meaning that the deepest, more purposeful life may not be one dedicated to an extraordinary cause or endeavor, but one that's simply lived with a deep sense of awareness and openness to both the known and the unknown. A passion for discovery, for embracing the new and the unfamiliar, can help you transform your life in ways you never dreamed possible, as you find the strength to move out of fear and resistance, and into something new.

Core Creativity and Mindfulness

Mindfulness helps you access your core creativity by making you aware of your resistance so that you can choose to let go of it and focus on the present moment. Right now, you might still be struggling with resistance and feeling unsure of your goals. Mindfulness allows you to tolerate the discomfort of not knowing what's next and to enter into the state of true originality and flow. When you've tapped into your core creativity, you'll discover that you don't feel the need to define your goals immediately. You trust that in time, you'll have clarity about where you want to go and how you might take your first steps in that direction. You can let go of any need to know exactly how you'll reach your goal and, instead, simply trust that all the steps on the path will reveal themselves eventually. The quality of spaciousness available to you in open mind lifts you out of the sense that you have to strictly define your parameters and dream "realistically." What once seemed unrealistic now seems possible (although you'll have to refine and hone your dream at a later point, which you'll learn about in part IV).

Too often, people lock themselves into a goal without taking the time to be mindful and let go of their urgency, which would allow them to connect to their passion and dream big. I've seen many clients begin dating almost desperately after a breakup, or sending out hundreds of résumés within days of losing a job. After receiving a dire health diagnosis, a client will plunge headfirst into a new plan of eating, exercising, and stress reduction, and spend hours researching her disease. There's nothing wrong with this sort of almost manic, immediate response to change. At first, it works well to alleviate the pain of suffering, of having to face the unknown and let go of what was familiar and comforting. But very soon, this attitude creates more discomfort. By letting go of any resistance to deeper change, you make yourself available for something much greater than you might have conceived of in a moment of anxiety.

After a loss, you need time to grieve and to slowly begin to formulate a plan. Core creativity, coupled with mindfulness, keeps you from frantically searching for the security of the known. It allows you to be present with your surroundings, to find your sense of grounding and purpose, and to reorient yourself and assess which direction you want to move in. Instead of being on the rebound, you can "recalculate your route" calmly as needed, just like a GPS system resetting itself after an unexpected turn.

THREE STATES OF CONSCIOUSNESS: WISE MIND, BIG MIND, AND OPEN MIND

In Buddhism, there are three states of consciousness, defined as wise mind, big mind, and open mind, which serve as metaphors for the stages we go through in the process of creative transformation. (I am using "wise mind" in the Buddhist sense, to denote a state of consciousness in which one transcends the unwholesome aspects of cognitive and egoic mind so that the sense of personal self drops away. Buddhists refer to this state of consciousness as "wise mind" or the "no self.")

In mindfulness meditation, you soon stop running with your thoughts wherever they take you, and find yourself sitting with a sense of serenity and clarity, observing what your mind churns up and easily discerning its qualities, setting aside what's unwholesome and taking delight in what's wholesome. In this state, called "wise mind," you easily and naturally sort through the thoughts, feelings, and sensations that enter your awareness, and let go of those that don't serve you.

After you've quieted all the busy activity of your mind, which tends to look forward into the future or backward into the past, and you've surrendered to the present moment, you may be able to experience what Buddhists call "big mind." In big mind, freed from the effort of concentrating or of noting and organizing thoughts, you're so absorbed in the moment that you experience a blissful oneness with all that is. If wise mind is the doorway to the house of self, where your core creativity resides, big mind is the entryway.

From big mind—or even sometimes directly from wise mind—you step into a state of core creativity, or what's called "open mind." In this receptive state, you feel a sense of spaciousness, timelessness, and willingness to entertain new possibilities. You're curious, nonreactive, compassionate, and accepting of the present experience, whether it's positive, negative, or neutral. Creative flow occurs here in the main part of the house of self.

These states of consciousness mirror the three steps in the art of creative transformation:

1. *Let go* into wise mind. By paying attention to your mind flow, you see all the thoughts and feelings that might distract you, but you're wise enough to simply let them go. Opening up, you become ready to tune in.

2. *Tune in* to big mind. As you tune in, you cease focusing on your breathing or your sorting process. All becomes quiet and serene as you melt into bliss, the waters of your consciousness undisturbed by feelings, thoughts, or sensations. In big mind, there's no individual "I" present. There's a vast, spacious, eternal, and pervading sense of pure, pristine awareness that allows you to move forward.

3. *Move forward* into open mind. You allow the creativity from your core to flow into you, sweeping you up and sending you in the direction of the unknown. Once you've experienced the mystical and transformative power of your core creativity, you can trust in its currents and let it send you downstream; though surrendering to it at first, you then gently steer it as you begin to recognize which way you'd like to go and remember that you have the power to direct your course.

BECOMING CREATIVELY TONED

Ordinary creativity helps you adjust to changing conditions and think your way out of problems, but core creativity offers infinitely more. It empowers you to pursue your passion enthusiastically even when faced with challenges. It helps you remain enthusiastic and resilient regardless of circumstances, because you've learned that you can always rely on this powerful force to lead you out of the woods of the unknown and into the clearing.

As I mentioned previously, just as working with free weights builds muscle, mindfulness practice builds mindstrength. Similarly, just as an athlete who's in condition has the muscle tone to be able to spring into action instantly, someone who regularly accesses core creativity through daily mindfulness practice becomes creatively toned. For this person, the faucet to this remarkable flow of inspiration opens up easily, naturally, and often, allowing spontaneous and dramatic breakthroughs.

Steve Jobs is an excellent example of someone who stays creatively toned so that he can access his core creativity. A regular meditator, he was once best known for designing the Apple computer. When he had a falling out with his own company, he bought Pixar, a movie studio started by George Lucas that had experienced some minor successes. Jobs was involved in developing their first two movies, both big hits that helped usher in a new era of animated feature films: *Toy Story* and *Toy Story 2*. Eventually lured back to Apple, Jobs introduced a new line of Apple computers, as well as iTunes, the iPod, and the iPhone, which furthered the trend of offering easier Internet downloading of music in the form of MP3 files (Deutschman 2000). Being creatively toned, as Steve Jobs is, can come about by accessing core creativity again and again.

When you're creatively toned, instead of merely dipping your toe in the water and playing it safe, you're willing to be utterly daring. Knowing this, you can navigate through a sea of self-limiting thoughts and transform such unwholesome beliefs as "I had my chance and blew it," "It's too late; my time is over," "I'll never be happy again," and "I can't." The clouds of negativity part and the light of possibility beams down upon you. Mindstrength helps you recognize that in each moment, you can choose to let fear determine your course or to let creativity direct you.

OVERCOMING THE INTIMIDATION FACTOR

If you've never experienced core creativity, or haven't since you were a child immersed in the magical world of your imagination, it may be hard for you to believe that you could be a true innovator in your life. Many people hold onto the unproductive belief that they aren't imaginative. Yet, if you think back to your early childhood, you'll probably recall that you had no such limiting belief. It didn't occur to you that you couldn't draw a masterpiece with your crayons or fashion a grand sculpture with Play-Doh. As you matured, your left brain and its rational, logical patterns of thinking began to dominate your right brain's more intuitive approach to understanding and perceiving. Meanwhile, any unresolved emotional traumas, small or large, affected your perception of yourself. The desire to be accepted by others caused you to conform to the expectations of the people around you.

While such behavior is adaptive for someone who's trying to find security within his social group, it cuts off the lifeline to nourishing core creativity. The mind develops a habit of quickly judging which behaviors the group will readily accept and which will be questioned or even ridiculed. The mind dismisses original thoughts before they have a chance to fully form. As a result, by young adulthood, most people have developed an unwholesome belief that they're not creative, as well as a fear of stepping out into the unknown. Averse to risk, they conform to the expectations of others.

Remember, creativity is about journeying into the dark and mysterious forest of the unknown. It's not necessarily about participating in the arts, although it can be. Years ago, the married woman who didn't have a paying job but took care of her husband's and children's needs introduced herself as "just a housewife," unknowingly communicating her belief that such a role couldn't possibly involve originality. "Housewives" later became "homemakers," as women, and even men, began to acknowledge that there was more to tending a home and caring for a family than simply being a "wife" in a "house." Now, many women, and men too, say that parenting and running a home can be creative work. Academy Award–winning actress Jodie Foster has been quoted as saying that parenting is the most creative thing she has ever done, which is an interesting comment on what constitutes a creative outlet and the experience of creativity.

Like the New York City taxi driver who understood that his job wasn't simply to transport me from point A to point B, you can let go of the idea that you're confined by the seemingly unalterable parameters of your life right now. You can begin opening the door to your core creativity and to open-mind awareness. You can stop yearning for the big chance to find a sense of purpose and start experiencing it today, regardless of the mundane items on your agenda.

One of my clients was a single mother who always looked to the next workshop or class to help her find enlightenment and purpose. She was frustrated, because her time and funds were limited, and she felt that she was far from discovering her passions and from experiencing contentment, joy, and enthusiasm in her life. She yearned for change but felt blocked from being able to do the work required to become a more mindful and contented person. I asked her what time of day she felt the most frustrated and the most distanced from a sense of purpose, and she told me that it was in the morning, when she had to rush to get her children off to school. I suggested that she practice being mindful during this hectic thirty-minute morning routine, putting into practice all the spiritual wisdom she'd learned so far. To her surprise, this thirty-minute mindfulness practice allowed her to discover ways to parent more originally. She took time to truly listen to what her children were communicating, not just verbally but with their body language and actions. She responded to them with curiosity and openness instead of the same old exasperated nagging. She was able to transform her anxiety about getting the children to school on time, and found herself automatically making adjustments to their morning routine to make it run more smoothly. She didn't have to think about what she might do to make this family time more pleasurable and stress free; the knowledge simply came to her. These are the sort of breakthroughs that you, too, can make as you become more creatively toned.

In a crisis, being creatively toned can help you avoid depression and a sense of paralysis and fear. You can simply enter the process of creative transformation, knowing that at the conclusion, you'll have moved forward into fashioning a new and satisfying mandala of your life.

ENHANCING EVERYDAY CREATIVITY

One of the most effective ways to become creatively toned and start accessing core creativity is through mindfulness practice. Mindfulness allows us to listen and pay attention to what we might otherwise overlook—whether it's a fresh idea or a new way of perceiving a situation—enhancing our creativity and letting go of our obstacles to innovation. I once sat in on a meeting of record company executives in which they tried to solve some problems the company was experiencing. I silently noted how often the attendees said no, shutting down inventiveness and exploration, versus how many times they said yes, opening themselves up to new possibilities. The ratio was about three to one. When I pointed this out to them halfway into the meeting, they were astonished. They had no idea how quickly they'd been dismissing ideas. Many times, a brainstormed idea seems unworkable on the surface, but if you become curious and open to thinking about and viewing a problem differently, you may discover options you hadn't considered.

Dabbling in the Arts

Our culture's overemphasis on fame and great success often turns people away from their creative inclinations, because they feel that if they can't reach a professional goal with their writing, singing, or painting endeavors, they shouldn't bother. What they don't realize is that simply dabbling in the fine arts, with no specific goals or intentions, awakens our ability to approach life with greater openness and curiosity. In the same way that mindfulness practice jogs the areas of the brain associated with well-being, optimism, and compassion for yourself and others, which we all need in a crisis, so too does immersing yourself in any artistic exploration or enjoyment jog your creativity.

I often encourage my clients to take an evening or weekend art class; to invest in a sketchbook and charcoal, and time spent drawing; or to write in a journal, letting their imagination guide them. I've found that even people who are active in the creative industries, whether as artists or executives in film or advertising, benefit from artistic dabbling. I'll encourage a professional writer to take a dance class or buy some acrylic paints and stretched canvas, and start painting. In fact, many famous, highly successful recording artists and actors have a "secondary art" they dabble in, because they know that by taking the pressure off themselves to produce something that's a marketable project, they can get their creative juices flowing without being intimidated by thoughts of inadequacy. Any sort of creative dabbling primes the pump and increases your ability to quiet the thoughts generated by the rational brain and pay attention to what the intuitive brain produces.

Working Mindfully with Dreams

If you feel that you simply have no creative abilities, consider your dreams. Most nights, your mind generates at least a few fantastical images that you can recall upon waking if you slowly bring yourself back into consciousness with the intent of remembering your dreams. I often ask my clients to work with the images of their dreams by meditating on them, writing about them, and exploring them to see what ideas and insights they have to offer. To do this, keep a notebook, a mindfulness journal, or tape recorder by the bed, and when you become aware of your dream, whether it's in the middle of the night or at first light, record with as much detail as possible the entire dream or whatever fragments, images, feelings, or emotions you can recall. Enter a state of quiet, mindful reflection and let the dream replay itself in your consciousness. Note that each symbol in the dream represents some aspect of yourself, so after recalling the dream, think about how, for example, the stairs, the landing, the shadowy and ominous figure that emerges from a room down the hall, the hallway itself, and so on represent some part of you.

Dreams serve both as symbolic representations of your inner world and messages about what's going on in your everyday world of work, home, family, and friends. To paraphrase Freud's general formulation, our dreams are the royal road to our unconscious.

Immersing Yourself in Nature

Experiencing nature can awaken in you a sense of vitality and infinity, which becomes a path to your core creativity. Without conscious thought, you can look up at the astonishing number of stars in the sky or leaves on a single tree in a forest, and feel a sense of vastness and spaciousness. As you gaze at the heavens the ancients observed, knowing that humanity throughout history and across continents has pondered these very stars, you experience being a part of something larger than yourself that feels as if it has always existed and always will.

Expansiveness, limitlessness, and abundance are all qualities that speak to the right brain, validating its understanding of our own nature. The self-limiting thoughts churned up by the rational mind become dwarfed by a sense that there are no boundaries to vitality and there are countless opportunities for creative rebirth.

Some of the most creative thinkers spent a great deal of unstructured time in nature in their formative years. It appears that many artists, philosophers, leaders, and thinkers throughout time have intuitively used mindful awareness to further their inner development.

In nature, the rules of time don't seem so rigid. If you meditate by a tall redwood, majestic willow tree, or wise old oak, you begin to develop an appreciation for mother nature's infinite amount of creativity. You become more trusting of the rhythm of change. Nature recycles, mulching the old, and renewing itself again and again. Your unconscious, intuitive mind will recall your own capacity for drawing strength and nourishment from the ground beneath you, the foundations of your skills, knowledge, relationships, and all that you've created for yourself. It will recall your ability to stretch upward into the sky, continually expanding and adding new branches to your experiences. It's one thing to recognize the lessons of nature and how they can enhance your own ability to embrace change, but entirely another to immerse yourself in it and actually experience your connection to a larger life force that offers the possibility of something new pushing through the soil and reaching upward.

Most of our time is spent living in man-made shelters, absorbing artificial light that disrupts our natural connection to nature's rhythms. You can micromanage your environment indoors, but the more time you spend outdoors, the more you'll trust in your ability to adapt to an ever-changing environment that's filled with surprises.

Entering Sacred Space

In ancient times, sacred spaces, such as churches, temples, and sites for group rituals, were built on land whose features evoked a sense of spirituality. Treks to places like Machu Picchu, the temples of India, and Stonehenge have become more popular for Westerners who yearn for a sense of connection to their divine nature. Yet sacred spaces can exist wherever you feel a sense of spaciousness and connection to the creative, life-supporting forces of the universe. Arranging the space in your home or office to bring in light and nature will help you feel expansive and access your core creativity as you open up to your important role in all of creation.

On one of my many journeys to India, I took a boat ride on the Ganges River at sunset near the sacred city of Varanasi, where Hindus go to scatter the ashes of their loved ones after death. I was instructed by a Vedic priest to bathe, wear all-white attire and a garland of flowers around my neck, and then bow three times—once for Brahma, the creator god; once for Vishnu, the preserver; and once for Shiva, the destroyer—as a death and rebirth ritual before entering the boat. At first, I felt a little awkward performing this foreign and cumbersome ritual, but when the boat left the shore and headed out into the early evening fog, I felt a sense of peace come over me, a still and pervading, mystical quietude unlike anything I had ever experienced. I was in awe at the beauty of the river and the night sky, and deeply touched by having undergone the simple ritual that set all of this into motion.

Seeking Out Creative Stimulation

When the Irish band U2 wanted to reinvent their music, they traveled to Berlin, a bustling, gritty city unfamiliar to them, and soaked in the atmosphere, allowing its energy to infuse their songwriting and sound. The Edge (lead guitarist Dave Evans) said that while in Berlin, he'd become curious about his dreams and fascinated with this complex inner world of new, vibrant, and creative sounds, whose source he wanted to explore more deeply (Evans 1993). Similarly, a famous actor I once spotted in an art museum stood before a painting for a good ten minutes before throwing his arms out and his head back, and standing for many more minutes, as if opening his heart to a beam of creative energy emanating from that painting. We all have this capacity to open to the vital forces around us and allow ourselves to take them in, mingling them with our own passions.

Most people have a vague, intuitive sense that when in crisis and wrestling with fears about the unknown, they can spark some ideas about what to do by changing the scenery. However, traveling to a different environment is less about getting away from your uncomfortable situation and hoping to discover a specific idea of what your next move should be, and more about allowing yourself to experience new ways of perceiving.

A museum or gallery, a store featuring beautifully designed everyday objects, or a theater or concert hall all offer obvious creative stimulation, but walking through any unfamiliar setting offers a chance to develop

145

trust in the new and unexplored. If you've ever vacationed in a spot you'd never visited before, you may have felt tentative about turning down a street and afraid of losing your bearings and getting lost. Maybe the next day, you remembered that the little shop you enjoyed was on a side street just past the bookstore, which provided a sense of increased confidence as you began to get a grasp of the terrain. This experience of entering the unknown, peering around its corners and into its crevices, and gaining a sense of familiarity awakens in your awareness your ability to learn something new and incorporate it into your knowledge. At the same time, it invites you to connect what you already know with what's fresh and unexpected.

For the members of U2, Berlin's unique atmosphere was at once quite different from their usual environs, and familiar enough that they weren't utterly lost and confused. They were able to step out of their comfort zone and open themselves up to the city's rhythms, colors, and moods, mingling them with their own creative juices and eventually producing a groundbreaking album, *Achtung Baby*. You don't necessarily have to travel to experience immersion in an unfamiliar world. Reading books or watching movies that transport you to a different time or place can trigger your creativity and openness to the unknown and unexplored in your own life. However, most of us have so many demands on our time that the temptation is to pause the movie or set aside the book again and again while attending to the details of our lives. To truly "get away," you may have to physically leave your environment, if only to travel a few miles away to an area unfamiliar to you that can spark a sense of wonder, curiosity, and possibility.

Mindful Movement

The Mevleviye, a Sufi order, are known as whirling dervishes ("spinning initiates") for their spiritual practice of spinning their way into a trancelike state. Many forms of physical movement can be an entrée into open-mind consciousness. Somatic therapy or somatic disciplines such as martial arts, tai chi, and yoga are the most well-known ways of quieting the rational mind and opening up to the intuitive mind and its connection to the numinous creative force. Any physical activity that involves discipline and a slowing down of thoughts, from skiing to dance, actually creates new neural pathways in your brain that become roads to innovation. The terms "runner's high" and "yogic bliss" refer to the release of endorphins, neurotransmitters that create a sense of calm and contentedness, which occurs when practicing ashtanga yoga, vinyasa flow, or power yoga, and when engaging in other forms of rigorous exercise. Yogic bliss and runner's high are both very close to a state of core creativity; in a sense, they're gateway drugs!

Mood Management

Physical activity raises the heart rate and causes a release of endorphins, alleviating depression in both the short and long terms. Depression is a loop of unwholesome thoughts, feelings, beliefs, and sensations that feed upon themselves, spiraling the sufferer downward and away from an experience of hope, joy, enthusiasm, or curiosity. It chokes off the pipeline to the creative core, making times of transition especially difficult to handle emotionally. Recent studies have shown that regular exercise is an effective mood enhancer and a useful aid in the treatment of depression.

Depression has a quality of contraction. When you're depressed, your mind generates distorted thoughts that become formidable roadblocks to creative transformation. Moderate (not clinical) depression caused by loss has a similar, although less extreme, effect. Finding love again, regaining your health or enthusiasm for life, or discovering new opportunities for a rewarding livelihood seems impossible when you're overwhelmed by grief, sadness, and fear. By physically opening up the channels for movement within the body—the pathways for lymphatic fluid movement, blood circulation, and transport of oxygen, as well as the flow of *chi*, what ancient Chinese medicine regards as our vital force—you open up the channels for core creativity to flow into your awareness and lift you out of moderate depression.

Not I, not I, but the wind that blows through me!
A fine wind is blowing the new direction of time.
If only I let it bear me, carry me; if only it carry me!...

—D. H. Lawrence, "Song of a Man Who Has Come Through"

Despite the help of psychiatric drugs, many who struggle with depression and mood swings have lost faith in the psychiatric community's ability to help them temper the intensity of their dark moods without dulling their lighter ones. Sarah, who had been suicidal before coming to me, said that the only thing that gave her some hope that therapy might work for her after years of failure was the fact that the doctors had told her she'd beaten the odds of survival. The sense that she'd been given a second chance at life instead of succumbing to the drug overdose inspired her to try therapy one more time and use psychiatric drugs to help her overcome her depression. However, it wasn't until she had a transformative breakthrough in mindfulness meditation and accessed her core creativity that she regained her faith in the process of psychological counseling.

Too often, people try to self-medicate and end up being less able to regulate their moods. If you want to open up to a sense that tomorrow will bring new situations, new people, and new ideas, eliminating unwholesome moods is very important, but you must be careful in how you go about it.

Mindfulness meditation, yoga practice, and regular exercise are all excellent for mood regulation, because they lower the levels of the stress hormone cortisol in your bloodstream, increase your interleukin levels (enhancing your immune system and providing you with greater energy), and streamline your body's ability to cleanse itself of chemical toxins, such as lactic acid in your muscles and bloodstream, which can affect neurotransmitter receptors and alter your mood (Chopra 1994; Rossi 1993). I always try to get a sense of whether or not my clients are using drugs or even food to manipulate their moods, and if so, I refer them to a nutritionist; a psychiatrist or psychopharmacologist; or a holistic doctor, such as an integrative medical doctor, to break this habit.

It's true that many musicians and artists use drugs, particularly mild hallucinogens such as hashish and marijuana, as tools for transforming their moods and tapping into their creativity. But over the years of counseling many such artists, I've come to the opinion that drugs are very rarely a good option and are never the best way, in the long term, to hook up to your creative core. You can open the doors of consciousness with drugs for a limited amount of time, but then the cost is too high. Even if you don't develop an addiction or empty your bank account while using them, you overstimulate the dopamine and norepinephrine receptors in your brain. In a sense, you burn them out so that everyday pleasures can't produce a positive, much less euphoric, feeling without resorting to drugs again. I've seen people become overstimulated by one drug, then start using another to reduce its side effects and help them sleep, leading to such a severe imbalance that it takes many months of correction to bring their systems back to balance.

I've also seen very creative people explore their creativity without drug use, then veer off course and start using drugs as a temporary window into open mind. They end up feeling depleted and unable to reaccess that deepest state of creativity.

Wholesome practices, such as the ones described in this chapter, are far more effective for opening yourself up to core creativity and becoming creatively toned. They aren't fraught with the danger of severe emotional crashes and chemical imbalance. In many ancient cultures, hallucinogenics were used ritualistically, with great restraint and respect. Using drugs as a quick transport is quite different.

Becoming Quiet and Doing Nothing

You don't have to "try" to be creative when you access core creativity. You don't have to "think through" what to do next, because a sense of possibility and wonder will simply come to you, followed by ideas that flow into you. By becoming quiet, you begin to tone yourself creatively as you allow your unconscious mind to open up. Ideas will start bubbling to the surface of your awareness, often in the form of images or a sense of deep, inner knowing. Even when you don't clearly see what you want to do next, you stop looking at your watch or thinking about how long it's taking to get an answer. In open mind, you enter into a space of not knowing and not doing, a sacred inner room in the temple of your soul's creative process where time slows down and you experience an abiding appreciation of silence as you wait patiently for your inner wisdom and awareness to speak to you.

Slowing down your activities and becoming quiet, cultivating a state of listening, and gaining access to the interior sanctum of the soul's creative self are part of most religious traditions. In Buddhist monasteries, monks go for weeks or even months without speaking. Jesus was said to have spent forty days in the desert praying and meditating. I've also known creative artists who spend several hours sitting in a room, surrounded by their painting supplies, staring at a canvas, as Jackson Pollock regularly did, remaining in silence and waiting for the flow of ideas. A world-class drummer once took me inside his music room, slowly moved his hand across the drum kit, and said, "Sometimes I sit here for hours in the silence and quietly wait for the drums to tell me what to write and play." As he spoke, I realized his ability to patiently wait and remain in an open, listening state was a key element in his ability to create amazing music.

But in a world that operates at a faster pace each year, we feel pressured to stay on our toes, thinking and planning, running from one activity to the next. We've lost the ability to completely immerse ourselves in a process of wonder and discovery. As children, we lost track of time while playing. Now, many schedule their lives in fifteen-minute intervals. Disruptions and distractions are everywhere, from our "smartphones" hounding us with text messages throughout the day to our e-mail demanding that we sign the latest petition.

What's more, a long retreat or vacation is unavailable to many, given the demands on their time. Yet the Buddha taught that it's the act of slowing down, becoming quiet, and opening up that's most important, not the amount of time spent on a meditation cushion. Twenty minutes, twice a day, spent in quiet awareness, resting the anxious activity of the monkey mind, tones us creatively.

When you're in crisis, your body's immune system may weaken to the point where you become ill and are forced to slow down and be quiet. You become acutely aware of your physical discomfort. You sleep more, accessing the world of your dreams. Rather than wait until your body forces you to retreat, you can actively choose to be in charge of this process of becoming quiet. If you do, you'll gradually open yourself to the possibility of fully experiencing your core creativity.

Your self-insight and psychological awareness give the experience of core creativity its context. Someone who has very little self-awareness and suddenly opens the doors of perception won't necessarily be able to use that experience to inform his understanding of himself or his life. A slow approach toward the threshold, achieved by working to become creatively toned and using the rational mind to make sense of your experiences, prepares you to do more than merely marvel at the rush of awareness that comes as a result of accessing an open-mind state.

As a result of your reverie and your conscious mind's understanding that, indeed, you were responsible for turning on this creative flow and you can do it again, you're forever transformed. You'll never forget your ability to break through to the deepest state of creativity.

PERSEVERING AND TRUSTING IN THE CREATIVE PROCESS

Although artists are often seen as flighty or undisciplined, in my experience the most successful ones are extremely disciplined. They may spend a workday seemingly doing nothing, but in fact, they're consciously choosing to remain in a state of openness. They'll often pick up a guitar and start playing anything, or sit at a computer and start typing whatever comes to mind, in order to start their creative flow. When nothing comes, they aren't afraid to shift gears, to take a walk or a long retreat, to pick up a pen instead of a guitar, to break the formula of how they've always chosen to connect to their creativity by trying something entirely different. Trusting that they'll tap into that flow, they persevere long past the point when others would give up.

The reason they're able to persevere isn't because they have a particular temperament, but because they've experienced breakthroughs again and again. They know that they can rely on two distinct channels to glide into that space where we can all access our core creativity: honing our craft, a left-brain activity that tones us creatively over time, opening one of these channels; and persevering and trusting in this art of creative transformation, which opens the other.

By using the three-step creative process of let go, tune in, and move forward, which mirrors the states of wise mind, big mind, and open mind, you develop your ability to trust that you can experience breakthroughs. You're able to persevere in your mindfulness practice, because you've seen the results and progress you've made. A new obstacle may temporarily hold you back, but your trust in the art of creative transformation will rise up quickly, allowing you to surrender to the unknown. You let the winds of change blow away the sands of your mandala, without giving in to fear. Then you can discover all the resources you have at hand.

CHAPTER 9

Discovering the Gold Within

My quest is paradoxical: the distant truth I seek lies hidden in
the motivation that sends me searching; though it impels me
outward toward the world, I must find a way to bend it back
upon itself, and make it illumine its origin.

—Allen Wheelis

Within each of us lies resources as hidden as a vein of gold buried deep within a mountainside. Your gold is your unique set of interests, talents, and skills, as well as your passions, yearnings, and capacity for experiencing well-being. Expressing your inner gold will give you a sense of joy and purpose.

The great opportunity in any crisis is that it can awaken you to your desire for meaning, for living more authentically, more vibrantly. Your inner gold consists of your resources for creating a new, more satisfying mandala.

YOUR INNER GOLD

Shame, embarrassment, and the unwholesome thoughts and feelings your mind generates can prevent you from perceiving that you possess valuable talents and skills. Many of my clients who've lost their live-lihoods or been left by their long-term partners experience a sort of amnesia, because they become mired in insecurities and have difficulty remembering all that they have to offer. Clients have also told me that they've "never" felt pride or confidence, nor can they recall any of their positive qualities that served them in the past.

By practicing mindfulness and building mindstrength, you'll be able to break through the hard rock that's hiding your vein of gold: the resis-tance, fear, and feelings of low self-worth. Doing the work of tolerating your painful feelings while setting aside the meaningless, unwholesome chatter of your mind allows you to cut through the rock, revealing your inner treasure.

When you think of talents or skills, you might imagine what you'd list on a résumé, but some of the most valuable assets can be less obvious: patience, reliability, flexibility, the ability to see the big picture or the fine details, the ability to communicate effectively with a variety of people, and so on. You may also have the gold of specialized knowledge, not just in your chosen professional field, but gathered from your life experi-ences. You might be street smart or know a lot about the habits of a par-ticular group of people or understand how to motivate others. Because we so often think only about skills that are marketable or talent that's exceptional, it can be easy to overlook your own gold, which can take many forms. Neglected and ignored, your treasures may be hidden in the shadows of your consciousness, blocked from view by the clutter of unwholesome thoughts, feelings, and self-judgments. To go back to our earlier example of being disorganized (see chapter 6), only after you've let go of any negative associations with the label "disorganized" can you see to the gold: flexibility, creativity, resilience, and so on.

One of the gifts of letting go of fear and resistance is that you start to develop more wholesome perceptions of yourself, and your eye begins to catch a glimpse of those veins of gold that you've been overlooking. You begin to see that you have many qualities, talents, and skills that can serve you. Some may have been lying dormant for years, forgotten, while others may never have emerged until now. You may not realize your capacity for patience until you have to deal with a parent who has dementia, or your capacity for creating close friendships with people until your spouse, who managed your social life and family relation-ships, is gone.

Very often, to avoid the discomfort of feeling inadequate, we develop the habit of delegating to others tasks that feel unnatural to us. Over time, it becomes harder to trust that we have the capacity to handle those challenges. In a crisis, when we need to reclaim our talents and skills, we can become blocked by fear.

You can use the following exercise to discover any hidden knowledge about yourself and the qualities you can draw upon to help you.

The Ideal House of Self Meditation

Sit quietly and mindfully, being aware of your breath as it rises and falls. Feel yourself opening up to your inner wisdom. Feel your awareness expanding. Let your curiosity arise.

Allow your hidden wisdom to reveal the image of your ideal house of self. What does your house look like? Is it spacious or intimate?

In your mind's eye, walk toward the front door of this ideal house, knowing that you own it. It's yours to explore, to learn from, to refashion in any way you choose. Place your hand on the handle of the door and open it, entering into the house of self.

What do you see? As you look around you, are there any images that speak to you?

Do you hear sounds or music playing? What do these sounds tell you? What does the music tell you? Do you hear song lyrics?

What do you feel?

Is anyone there to greet you? Who is this wise figure? A teacher or healer? Someone who can offer you insight? Is this person speaking to you, either with words or body language?

Listen carefully. Observe. Take in all that you hear and see.

Walk through all the rooms of the house. Notice your surroundings. Pay attention to the feelings and sensations that arise as you walk through your ideal house of self.

- *What do you notice about each room?*
- *What do you hear?*
- *What do you see?*
- *What do you feel?*

✤ What are you experiencing?

Remain in a state of awareness, taking in all that this house has to tell you, until you're ready to end your meditation.

As you walk through your ideal house of self, your unconscious mind may decide that this is a good time to reveal something to you, and you'll have an unsettling or unpleasant experience in one of the rooms. Although your intention is to discover the gold, you may discover something else that you can transform into gold. If so, observe the cluttered, garbage-strewn room or the broken flooring, and as you do, notice the feelings and sensations that arise in you. Then, replace or fix this symbol: imagine yourself clearing away the clutter, replacing the floorboards, and so on. Relish the feeling of having corrected the flaws in your ideal house of self. After you end the meditation, explore what those images of brokenness and clutter represented for you. You may wish to write in your mindfulness journal about what you've discovered, noting exact details of everything that you experienced so that you can come back to it later and contemplate it some more.

REDISCOVER YOUR CAPACITY TO EXPERIENCE JOY AND OTHER WHOLESOME EMOTIONS

After you've developed mindstrength, you'll be better able to tolerate the suffering associated with grief and loss, and then recapture joy, a sense of pride, a loving connection with your partner, and so on. Rather than focus on the emotions you already know you want to experience again, dig a little deeper. Explore what once was, so that you can reclaim the qualities that will help you be resilient and create something new. You may rediscover your ability to feel a sense of community, which you've been missing so long that you can't even remember the last time you experienced it. You might rediscover your adventurousness, playfulness, or confidence and your capacity to love. Work with the ideal house of self meditation, as well as the following meditation, which will help you reclaim your forgotten ability to experience a range of wholesome emotions.

Recapture Wholesome Emotions

Return to a location where you've had very positive experiences. It may be a place you associate with being comfortable, enthusiastic and eager, appreciated and loved, or successful. It could be a place from your past: the park where you ate your brown-bag lunch every day when you were beginning your career, or a library where you spent countless hours as a child lost in the world of ideas and books. Any place with positive associations for you will work for this exercise.

Take a comfortable seat and begin to breathe mindfully, keeping your eyes open. Allow yourself to experience the wholesome emotions and sensations that arise for you. Let your observing mind label them as you bask in these energizing feelings (for example, acceptance, harmony, enthusiasm, and contentment).

Feel a sense of belonging. Be mindful and fully present with all that's around you. Don't allow your thoughts to take you elsewhere. Even if the place has changed since you first came there years ago, allow yourself to feel a sense of connection to it. You may want to close your eyes and imagine it exactly as it once was. Remember how you used to feel when you were there, and experience those emotions right now, in the moment.

When you've luxuriated in these enriching emotions, note what you've just experienced. Then ask yourself:

- *Which of these emotions can serve me right now?*

- *How can these emotions serve me?*

- *What have I discovered about myself? Have I discovered a forgotten ability? (For instance, had you forgotten that you could feel a particular emotion?)*

You may wish to write your answers in a mindfulness journal. You might also want to repeat this exercise several times, performing it in different locations.

Sometimes, the gold within is hidden because we haven't had the opportunity to discover it. Many of us have limited life experiences, and may take years to discover talents and passions we didn't know we had. Traveling, taking courses or workshops, attending lectures, and reading books are all ways to expose yourself to ideas and emotions you haven't experienced before, facilitating the process of self-discovery. Any of the exercises in chapter 8 that focus on creative stimulation will help you discover your passions and become creatively toned, connecting you to your core creativity.

WHOLESOME YEARNINGS

You experience wanting mind when you're out of step with the core values of your real self, and seeking from a place of dissatisfaction rather than from a desire to have more of what you authentically value. A wholesome desire stems not from discontent but a yearning for new challenges and fulfillment, and inspires you to take positive, productive action. The qualitative difference between wanting mind and wholesome yearning is significant. The former often occurs when your life is out of alignment with your authentic values. It cuts you off from your core creativity, causing you to generate unwholesome thoughts, feelings, and behaviors, such as hopelessness, judgment, despair, anger, and frustration. In contrast, the latter inspires enthusiasm, openness to possibility, and a feeling of optimism and expansiveness; it's a form of gold. You cannot engage in the three-step process of creative transformation when you're stuck in wanting mind, whereas wholesome yearning can launch you into it.

If you're experiencing wanting mind, you can transform its quality by taking your focus away from the lack and placing it on what you most desire. Rather than allow your mind to generate unwholesome thoughts that exacerbate your unwholesome feelings, meditate on those feelings, fully experiencing them and observing how they slowly dissipate. Then you can discover the gold within: the wholesome desire for a romantic partnership, a fulfilling livelihood, a sense of connection to others, and so on. Denied, these desires born of wanting mind cause frustration, anger, and depression, but acknowledged, they can become the impetus for designing and creating a new and far more fulfilling mandala of life.

DEALING WITH A SENSE OF LACK

In our culture, where individualism is so highly prized, many people feel pressured to stand out from the crowd and do something extraordinary. Announcement of an upcoming high-school reunion can cause people to feel ashamed and inadequate, because they see it as a reminder of how ordinary and unimportant they feel. It's easy to become far too identified with your accomplishments and start believing that if you're not number one, not successful in ways that your peers recognize, or not doing something unique, your life doesn't have much meaning. The quest for not just success but tremendous success, not just happiness but complete bliss at all times, can be debilitating, causing feelings of fear, hurt, and resentment, and blocking you from discovering what you might create for yourself.

You have to identify the lack or void and better understand it if you want to fill it. You may want to try counseling, coaching, journal writing, or workshops to explore this sense that something's missing. Although you're likely to experience some suffering when you finally acknowledge what you lack, you can then create a wholesome hunger and passion for developing that quality. You may not have the time, money, or freedom to do what you most desire, but if you acknowledge and accept your present reality, you'll find ways to open up time, expand your financial options, and free yourself from obligations you've mistakenly assumed can't be delegated or discarded.

I've often found that when my clients have done the work of establishing a mindfulness practice and building mindstrength, the discovery that they lack the skills or time to dedicate to a passion doesn't make them feel depressed or overwhelmed. Instead, they start to recognize possibilities for gaining those skills, and they begin to develop them. They're optimistic, and their ability to focus and be mindful of avoidance behaviors and distractions causes them to use their time more wisely. If they previously would have frittered away twenty minutes engaging in an unimportant, mindless activity, they now use that time pursuing their passions, even if in a small way, such as doing research, composing an e-mail, conversing with a mentor, and so on. They start to recognize the next step on the path.

Sometimes, the next step reveals itself in the smallest of moments. You might suddenly have an opportunity to deconstruct your old story of being shy and uncomfortable in large groups and, for the first time, find the courage to speak up in front of an audience about something that matters to you. The old habit of avoiding confrontation stops being an obstacle as you find yourself asking an old friend to explain a comment you found hurtful. Developing mindstrength makes accessing your courage far easier, and as you sail the ship of self into the unknown, you feel confident that you're headed in the right direction.

THE HIDDEN GOLD REVEALED BY INTUITION

An unusual aspect of core creativity is that it awakens your intuition, allowing you to access the gold of hidden knowledge by improving your capacity to be reflective and receptive. Being reflective gives you access to information in your unconscious mind that's hidden from your conscious mind. It lets you receive subtle communication. For instance, you may feel a sense that something's not right when you're offered a job you want or when you receive advice from a medical specialist. With mindfulness, you resist the temptation to set aside your discomfort and forge ahead; instead, you remain present with that feeling, allowing it to rise into your awareness. Then you explore where it's coming from. When you've honed your ability to easily access core creativity, you'll soon find that your intuition has become a trustworthy source of information, and you may not feel the need for hard evidence to validate it.

Another way intuition works is more mysterious, but after years of practicing mindfulness and cultivating my ability to experience core creativity, I've learned to trust it. At times, our intuition can greatly enhance our receptivity, allowing us to become aware of hidden knowledge that's not in our own unconscious but someone else's, or the collective unconscious.

I once counseled a woman named Elaine who had come to me for help in figuring out whether to remain in her marriage or leave her husband for a man she'd recently met. She was at a major turning point in her life and was afraid of making the wrong decision.

After our initial interview, I knew this second relationship was not for her. I also intuited that her relationship dilemma was not the main reason she'd come to me, although that's what she claimed. I told her, "I don't usually share something like this with someone I'm meeting with for the first time, but this unsettling feeling has come over me, and I sense that we should do something creative, and experiment." I asked her to meditate with me and enter a state of mindful awareness. She agreed, and almost immediately, an image appeared in my mind. I sat with it for a good twenty minutes as she and I continued meditating, and the image became sharper, creating in me a sense that it was very important to mention.

I said, "I don't know why, but I'm seeing an image of a young woman running along a road in the moonlight, shouting frantically. Can you think of why this picture might be appearing in my mind?"

Elaine was so shocked that she could hardly speak at first. Then, her voice cracked as she said, "I can't believe you're seeing that." In a shaky voice, she began to tell me about a memory she hadn't allowed herself to think about for decades. As a teenager, she'd been driving down a country road with her best girlfriend, when a deer appeared in front of them, causing her to swerve and crash the car into a tree. She immediately realized that her friend in the passenger seat was pinned in and unconscious, so she couldn't free her. Elaine ended up running down the road, shouting as she searched frantically for another car or a house where she could find help. By the time the ambulance arrived, her friend was dead. Afterward, the community was in such pain that her parents told Elaine she shouldn't contact her friend's family, or go to the funeral or the memorial service hosted by their school, and admonished her to never speak of the incident again.

This unusual surfacing of a long-repressed childhood memory jump-started our therapy, as we began to explore the emotions created those many years ago when Elaine was denied a chance to grieve her friend's passing and share that grief with others. She started to recognize that there she was, on the brink of a major life decision, having completely overlooked the main issue that had driven her to have an affair: her unresolved guilt had caused her to develop a deep sense of unworthiness, a sense that she didn't deserve a good marriage and family life. Instead of addressing her feelings of guilt and unworthiness, she'd unconsciously chosen to jeopardize her marriage and had chosen a new partner who was inappropriate for her.

I believe that the reason I was able to tap into Elaine's unconscious memory is because mindfulness practice awakens dormant abilities of the brain and enhances our underdeveloped abilities. Intuition, once a crucial tool for primitive human beings in determining the location of the wild-animal herds or which plants served as effective medicine for illness, is one of our lost skills. When we're at a crossroads and in need of greater wisdom and awareness, intuition can bring them in, allowing us to see more possibilities than our conscious mind can perceive. Had I thought to ask Elaine if she had any memories of past traumas that might have caused her to have difficulty with emotional intimacy, she probably wouldn't have been able to access that memory of the auto accident and its aftermath. After bringing it into our conversation, I was able to direct her into letting go of her old beliefs, tuning in to what she most desired, and moving forward, without having to rely solely on our "figuring out" what she should do. In time, she ended the affair and became more deeply committed to her marriage.

DISCOVERING WHAT YOU MIGHT SPIN INTO GOLD

As you become more creatively toned and open through using mindfulness and enhancing everyday creativity, you also become more tolerant of uncomfortable truths, because you've learned that you can manage the emotional pain of discovering them, extracting what's of value, and mulching them.

This forgotten knowledge may not seem like gold, because it causes you pain when you rediscover it, but it can be extremely valuable in helping you create a new vision for your life. This information often surfaces once you've established a mindfulness practice, because on some level, you recognize that you're ready to handle painful memories of the past or painful thoughts about what's happening in your life right now.

The memories that arise in your mind may seem suspect. Exploring whether or not they're literally true may not be all that important. However, it's important to discover the feelings, images, sensations, and thoughts that accompany the memories. Memories can become distorted over time, but the feelings that accompany them have their own truth. Memory is selective, and if an image of the past is suddenly arising in your consciousness, there's probably a reason for it—but it might not be the one you think.

Let's say that while meditating, you access a memory of yourself as a child: *you're visiting Chinatown with your grandmother on Chinese New Year, when you both step back in surprise as firecrackers suddenly explode at your feet in front of the store you're exiting.* At first glance, it's an arbitrary image of fear. However, as you relive the memory, allowing it to remain present in your awareness, you may discover that it doesn't have a quality of fear or danger, but of excitement and adventure. You might recognize that as a child, you learned from your grandmother that indulging in a sense of curiosity and adventure leads to pleasurable discoveries and a sense that anything can happen. But as an adult, you've forgotten your ability to take risks and explore, and now your mind is telling you that it's time to step out and try something new, even though there may be some danger involved. The more creatively toned you are, the easier it is to discover what lessons you can mine from the images and memories your mind brings into the light of your awareness.

Awareness that's currently hidden from the conscious mind may also start to appear in your dreams. A client of mine, a surgeon, had entered therapy because he was agonizing over his discomfort with his job. He had always loved operating but had developed an inexplicable feeling of dread when going to work and didn't know why. One day, he described to me a nightmare he'd had, in which he was driving a car that was speeding down a hill toward a brick wall; he hit the brakes, but the car wouldn't stop. He'd woken up just before it crashed into the wall. The surgeon was quite disturbed by the dream and the sense of powerlessness it engendered in him. I asked him to meditate with me, and guided him through the dream again, asking him to embody and give a voice to each object in the dream—the car, the brakes, and the wall—because each symbol in our dreams represents an aspect of the self. As the car, he felt he was veering out of control, which made him feel anxious and scared. As the brakes, he felt powerless and angry that the car continued to move forward at an alarming speed, and he also felt frightened of crashing and getting hurt. As the wall, he felt that he was endangering himself, that once the car hit, disaster would ensue.

As we went through this gestalt dream exercise several times, it suddenly occurred to him what these symbols meant: that he should listen to his instincts and cancel a surgery he was scheduled to do with another physician he'd never worked with before. A week after he'd successfully performed the rescheduled surgery with another member of the medical team, the one he'd been concerned about was fired for showing up to a surgery while under the influence of narcotics. This team member had previously shown no detectible signs of drug addiction, but clearly, my client's intuition had influenced his dream. My client went on to work at a different hospital where he felt more in control over choosing his team.

WORKING WITH INTUITION TO DISCOVER REAL GOLD, NOT FOOL'S GOLD

When you're first establishing a mindfulness practice, your intuition probably won't be very well honed. Unbeknownst to you, your gut feeling may come not from inner awareness but from inner resistance. In this case, you'll need to explore it mindfully to ensure that you've mined for real gold, that is, true insights and knowledge, and not fool's gold, thoughts generated by the ego.

Ask for help from a therapist, mentor, or wise partner from your wisdom council of support, someone who encourages you to slow down instead of being reactive. In this way, you can be certain that you're accessing reliable information rather than a distortion created by fear, resistance, and the desire for a quick fix. The more you feel a sense of urgency and anxiousness, the more important it is to sit and mindfully explore the information before acting on it. Often, people make bad decisions on the rebound after a loss, because in their anxiety, they put too much faith in their initial positive reaction to a new course of action, mistaking it for intuition, and refuse to explore it in depth. The romantic partner you've met once and are convinced is "the one," the moneymaking opportunity you've learned few details about, and the healer who promises a full cure for all your suffering are likely to disappoint you. You'll save yourself much heartache if you consult with a wisdom council of support that's filled with people who are willing to brave your defensive posturing and push you to slow down and explore your decision to take a particular road. At the same time, the more you practice mindfulness, the sooner you'll be able to recognize when you're operating from panic and fear instead of true intuition.

WISDOM COUNCIL OF SUPPORT

Seek help from a therapist, mentor, or wise partner from your wisdom council of support, someone who encourages you to slow down instead of being reactive.

If someone confronts you with a painful possibility—for instance, telling you that you seem to be acting out of anger, vindictiveness, or impulsive desires to accomplish goals without proper preparation—slow down and take in what this person is saying. The following exercise will help you explore whether what you're hearing is true and whether your "intuition" is false.

Sort Out the Fool's Gold

If you've been told by a trusted advisor that your intuition seems to be off, and that you're in an unwholesome state of thinking and feeling, ask yourself the following questions, bringing an attitude of curiosity and openness to each question. Remember, no one's perfect, so don't be ashamed of any unwholesome qualities that come forth as a result of making these inquiries:

- *If I were in this particular unwholesome state, how would I behave? What would I say and do? How would I react if someone confronted me about my anger (or jealousy, vindictiveness, dishonesty, and so on)? (You may want to meditate on that unwholesome quality, allowing yourself to experience it, before asking yourself this question.)*

- *Am I behaving as I would if I were angry (or jealous, vindictive, and so on)? Is there an unwholesome quality to my feelings? My thoughts? My actions? Am I experiencing a rigid, heavy, contracted feeling in my body?*

❧ *What are three reasons why I might be angry, impulsive, reactive, or jealous?*

Allow the truth to rise up into your awareness, and remember that any suffering it causes you will soon disappear as you use your insight to mine for the gold of this revelation.

If you discover that what you're experiencing might be fool's gold, but you're not sure, you can explore it further by gathering evidence that it is or isn't true. Let's say that you think your partner's angry with you, although she denies it. Ask her to explain why she behaved in a way that made you think she was angry (for example, she slammed a door or spoke in a sharp tone of voice). If she responds that you've interpreted her behavior incorrectly and she has a plausible excuse, be mindful of how you feel as she issues her denial. Do you feel confident that your intuition was wrong and you misinterpreted the situation, or do you still feel a sense of danger, threat, uneasiness, or discomfort? Trust this reaction, even if you can't justify it rationally. You may not be able to gather any more information immediately, but you can make note of what you've felt and experienced, and use it to inform you in the future.

Be mindful of your dreams and intuitive experiences, and listen to what they have to tell you. When you've honed your intuition and your ability to connect to your core self, you'll have greater courage, insight, and awareness of your resources, passions, and wholesome yearnings. Next, you can begin formulating your new vision in a flexible way, opening yourself to the widest range of possibilities for happiness.

PART IV

Move Forward: Practical Steps for Sailing Forth into the Unknown with Trust, Faith, and Enthusiasm

CHAPTER 10

Creating Your Mandala

*Never forget that life can only be nobly inspired and rightly
lived if you take it bravely and gallantly, as a splendid
adventure in which you are setting out into an unknown
country, to meet many a joy, to find many a comrade, to win
and lose many a battle.*

—Annie Besant

Having come this far in the art of creative transformation, you're ready
to envision a beautiful mandala that encapsulates your interests, desires,
wholesome qualities, talents, and purpose. Because you've learned to
tune in to your core creativity and practice mindfulness, the vision you
formulate will come from your heart instead of your head. Consequently,
you'll be able to maintain your passion for achieving it even when you're
faced with obstacles or feel unsure of the next step to take. Having
discovered your unique set of talents, skills, proclivities, and wholesome
longings, and learned to quiet the chatter of the mind that takes in far
too much feedback from outside of you, you'll find it's not so difficult to
distinguish between true passions and urgings from your false self.

Whatever mandala you fashion, know that it will be impermanent,
because change is inevitable. Recognizing that you have the ability to
alter your vision or create a new one at any point will give you the confidence to move forward. You should also know that yours won't be the
only hand to arrange the colored sands. You must formulate a flexible

vision that's true to your core self as well as realistic and achievable, given that you don't have control over all the circumstances that will affect how your vision manifests.

When you're in open mind, accessing core creativity, most anything seems possible. You dream big. You may not see any of the details of how this dream will manifest, but you know what your core self is calling you toward. Allow yourself to spend time being mindfully aware of why that dream means so much to you. When you let yourself believe that the impossible can be made possible, you empower yourself to discover all the opportunities available to you. From there, you can begin honing your vision to make it conform even more closely to what you want for yourself.

SHARPENING YOUR VISION

Initially, the vision or goal that comes to you may be short on details. Several years back, one of my clients, who worked in the music business, told me he could see that the industry was dramatically changing and that very soon, his job would be obsolete. He'd worked his way to the top of his profession, and now, he realized he would have to leave behind the rewarding career he loved.

As he worked with me to begin envisioning a new mandala, all he knew was that he wanted to live in a particular city. He'd only visited it a handful of times, but it felt like home to him. He started to explore what he might do if he lived there, took a few weeks to spend time familiarizing himself with the place, and realized that he could use his promotional skills, which had benefited so many musical artists, to promote a new business as an event planner. It took him time to get to know the venues and vendors, and he had to start by taking a low-paying sales job and living off his savings while he established himself. Because he practiced mindfulness, he didn't become distracted by the challenges of his sales job, was able to tolerate his anxiety about having to live very frugally, which he wasn't used to, and found ways to enjoy the city inexpensively.

Your vision may be a specific goal, but rather than make it an end point, imagine how you might feel connected to your goal today. Open yourself up to its taking a different form than you might expect. Perhaps your vision for yourself is to regain your health, stamina, and sense of well-being. As you move forward, struggling with a medical crisis, you're bound to have days when your vision of yourself easily climbing a steep hill as you walk your dog feels unattainable. Yet if you focus on the core of your vision, you'll start to see how you can create well-being even if your body isn't cooperating with your desire to feel healthy and strong today. Remaining mindfully aware of the strength you do have—not just your physical strength, but your mindstrength—will give you the courage to continue striving while remaining open to how your vision plays out. If you start to realize that your goal has to be adjusted, mindstrength will allow you to be honest about the situation and act accordingly instead of feeling disappointed and angry about what you can't achieve.

Your vision may be of living more authentically, loving more deeply, and having a more emotionally intimate relationship with your partner. You may want to parent more compassionately or feel more connected to the people in your life. You may yearn for all of these. By remaining mindful, you can work toward your goals every day, seizing every opportunity that appears. Your goal of balancing work and family life won't feel like something you'll only be able to accomplish down the road when the circumstances of your life change. Rather, you'll naturally make the decision to remain present with your family instead of pondering some issue that came up at work, or to be fully present while working instead of feeling guilty about not spending enough time with your family. With very little effort or emotional agitation, you'll be able to quickly make decisions that you used to agonize over.

Every goal requires persevering, learning something new, and being open to the unexpected. It also requires that all-important first step in getting started: making a plan.

GETTING STARTED: CREATING A REALISTIC VISION

As much as I like to encourage people to dream, and I believe the can-do spirit can carry them a long way, we all must accept certain realities. I've had clients who wanted to become professional performers, but when I've pointed out some of the requirements for being a successful performer in today's music or film industries, they've sometimes become defensive and argued that by sheer willpower, they could break all the rules and bypass "paying their dues." Sometimes that's true, but not usually.

Creating a realistic goal based on your vision requires learning more about what it typically takes for someone to reach that goal and being honest with yourself about how devoted you are to reaching it. Even a goal that's as simple as achieving balance in your life requires self-inquiry and self-honesty. You have to explore what would constitute balance for you, what skills you'd need to create that balance, and how you might acquire those skills. Ask yourself, "Do I really have the commitment and resources to follow through, or will I easily give up and slip back into the old ways?" At first, in your enthusiasm, you might feel certain you have enough passion to carry you past every obstacle. However, by now, having cultivated your observing self and built mindstrength, you know that you won't achieve your goal unless it's in sync with the passions of your core self.

Let's say your goal is to live a more balanced life, and you feel that to do that, you can't work more than a certain number of hours a week. Yet you can't imagine how you might work fewer hours and still meet your financial goals. You must face and resolve this conflict rather than hope it'll go away. Fortunately, once you've learned to let go of your resistance to change and set aside your unwholesome self-judgments, as well as your need to control every aspect of how your mandala unfolds, you'll find that there are more paths open to you than you once would've imagined. Your first step is to begin researching where they are and what sort of obstacles you might face.

THE RESEARCH AND SELF-INQUIRY STAGE

Any plan or vision requires research if you want to make it a reality. We've all known people who made a major move too quickly, without thinking through the details, because they were so eager to meet their goals. The novice monk seeking enlightenment enters the monastery on his first day, and is immediately shown a pile of potatoes in the kitchen and told to start washing and peeling them. Research and self-inquiry, which lay the groundwork for transformation, aren't always enjoyable and can be very time consuming, but you, too, must peel some potatoes to begin.

It's easier now than ever to gather information, yet with so many facts and opinions available, it can be very difficult to sort through it all without going into information overload. Search the Internet for a simple, standard recipe, and you're likely to find a dozen variations. You can become bogged down by all the possibilities. Mindfulness practice helps you slow down and recognize the difference between when you're compulsively researching just to ease your anxiety about the unknown and when you actually need more information.

You might also choose to check a specific, limited number of resources, for instance, reading three books on a topic you know you need to learn more about, or interviewing five people who've successfully made the transition you seek to make. When you recognize the same themes coming up repeatedly, you'll know you have a handle on the basics and can scale back your research.

What Financial and Other Resources Do You Need?

Quite often, my clients begin the process of envisioning a new mandala by insisting that they need more money. If you feel this way, explore this idea mindfully. Do you truly require a higher salary, and if so, is it realistic to expect to be paid more for your work? Can you reach your goals by living more frugally, and if so, how might you save money? Can you create passive income, that is, money that comes to you without your having to work by the hour for it (for example, through investments, royalties on an intellectual property, or rental property)? What does "more money" represent to you? Is money the resource you most need, or do you have an even greater need for creativity, flexibility, knowledge, courage, passion, or something else? Instead of assuming that money is your golden ticket to a fulfilling life, think about how you can increase the number and range of opportunities available to you. Too often, I've seen people direct their efforts into making more money, only to be disillusioned when it doesn't make them feel any happier.

Financial advisor Suze Orman's story illustrates how we can mistake money for the key to happiness. She came from a working-class, immigrant background; had a BA in social work; and was waiting tables in a bakery when a customer offered to invest fifty thousand dollars in her dream of starting her own business. She was thrilled, but as it turned out, having an infusion of money wasn't the ticket to a fulfilling career for her. She entrusted the money to a stockbroker who lost all of it in the market, and realizing that it would take years to earn that amount of money as a waitress, Orman opened her mind to other possibilities. She decided to enter a training program for account executives at Merrill Lynch. There, she gained greater knowledge about how to generate and manage finances, went on to establish her own financial services company, and, eventually, combined her knowledge of people and finances to create a niche for herself. The financial loss that could have devastated her, instead, inspired her to acquire the resources she needed to meet her personal and financial goals, and envision a mandala she might never have considered. Today, she says she works for the pure joy of it (Andriani 2003).

Learning by Example

Learning about how people have overcome obstacles and achieved success can help you identify the elements in their winning formulas, but then you must apply their insights and advice to your own life. By remaining creatively toned and in touch with the passions of your core self, you'll find it much easier to see the possibilities for using what they've learned to construct your own winning formula. Successful people often cite reliance, perseverance, support from others, discipline and a structured plan, and a clear vision of what they wanted to create in their lives as vital elements that kept them on track, but learning exactly how they got around certain obstacles and dealt with their frustrations and fears can give you some guidance.

TOLERATING THE LEARNING CURVE

Some meditation teachers insist that you must spend years on the meditation cushion before you can come anywhere near to experiencing a dissolution of the ego and accessing your core self (although, as mentioned earlier, the latest evidence proves otherwise). Others claim you need no formalized training whatsoever to reach this state, that you just sit and relax into it. Perhaps the latter works for some, but it doesn't for most. The egoic mind would love to believe in instant enlightenment and quick fixes. We'd rather not suffer through hard work or drudgery. Years ago, when I took piano lessons, I would arrive at the practice room and immediately start improvising, but my teacher would open the door, interrupt me, and scold me for not playing my scales. At first, I resisted her chiding, but then she reminded me that as a meditation teacher, I don't ask my students to come in, sit on the cushion, and "improvise." I had to admit that I was avoiding the scales because I wanted to fast-forward to the "good part."

One of my clients, Arianna, who had a trust fund, had recently divorced and was determined to become a day trader. She had only worked in part-time jobs that she felt held little prestige, and believed that making money in the stock market would not only be exciting but also give her a sense of power and accomplishment, and prove to her ex-husband, a high-powered executive, that she could be as successful as he was. She'd learned enough about day-trading to feel that she could become quite good at it, and she was eager to begin—too eager, I felt. I urged her to interview five successful day traders and ask them how they started and what advice they had for a beginner. Arianna followed through with this assignment but didn't like what she heard from all five people: they insisted that she start small, perhaps with five hundred dollars, and take at least three years to learn day-trading before investing more money than she could afford to lose. Undeterred by the day traders' words of caution, or mine, she ran through her entire trust fund and ended up living in her sister's extra room, feeling devastated by her losses.

Borrowing money to live on and starting to work full-time for the first time in her life, she continued seeing me for therapy and began working through the emotional issues that had led her to act too quickly on her vision. Through mindfulness, she was able to see that the problem wasn't her vision but her unwillingness to devote enough time and effort to building up her skills. Eventually, she did become a quite successful day trader and paid back those who'd helped her out financially, but she'd learned a painful lesson about the importance of research and self-evaluation.

We live in a culture that actively fosters the belief that you can skip right over the boring or difficult aspect of the change process, zip right through the learning curve instead of laboring at its beginning, and proceed directly to a contented state in which you're standing on solid ground, feeling completely secure and happy. We read about young people who had an idea for an Internet business and made a fortune before turning twenty-five. Their successes are exciting, but moving this quickly without "paying your dues" often doesn't work out quite so well. I've had several young clients who came into fame and fortune at an early age and were completely unprepared to handle it. If you try to rush to the "good part," you may have difficulty handling the sudden change, or you may land in a rebound job or relationship that's deeply problematic. In fact, you're likely to discover that the new situation has all the negative characteristics of the one you just left.

Out of the discipline of practicing mindfulness, cultivating the witnessing mind, and distinguishing between the wholesome and the unwholesome, you develop a foundation for improvisation and discovery. You're not so likely to follow the call of the ego and desiring mind instead of the call of the core self. Instead, you discover patience as you experience how it feels to engage fully in a process by pressing forward, even if you're bored, and resisting shortcuts.

Overall, I believe that most people are lulled into thinking that they have more expertise, more mastery, than they actually possess, because they want to avoid the pain of having to face the unknown and start at the beginning of a learning curve. Parents sometimes think that having had two or three children makes them quite skilled at parenting, but then they're flummoxed by the next child, whose needs and responses are very different from those of her siblings. Rushing into a situation can be avoided more easily if you're willing to tolerate the discomfort of being at the bottom of a learning curve.

I've found that even the most masterful musicians and songwriters say they have much to learn. They reach a certain level of expertise and then suddenly realize just how much they don't know, and they feel inspired all over again. When we open ourselves up to the possibility that we have to go back to beginner's mind, we open ourselves up to a personal transformation that may take great effort and be very frustrating, but ultimately turns out to be very rewarding, because it can lead to the most brilliant breakthroughs.

Creative artists spend a lot of time achieving mastery in their respective arts, and the results draw admiration from all corners. If you've never experienced mastery in any area of your life, you may not realize that it has its own gifts beyond what you're able to produce or accomplish. Mastery of any art or discipline helps you become more comfortable with the process of struggle, because you develop patience and trust as you craft, hone, and persevere. You're able to move easily between crafting and entering into a state of open mind, where you access core creativity to further guide you. This back-and-forth between focused effort and receptivity is the very nature of the process of creative transformation. The path through the woods is never straight and narrow, but winding; sometimes it's confusing and exacerbating, and at times, it opens up to a clearing where you feel that anything's possible and where you can dwell for a time before setting off again. You may not need to actually master new skills in order to set off in a new direction, but mastering mindfulness will build your patience and perseverance, and help you trust in the process of creative transformation.

WORKING WITH A VISION BOARD OR VISUAL REMINDERS

If you know what you need to do, or at least have a good idea about what your steps should be, visual reminders may help keep you on track. You might want to work with a vision board you create on your computer with the drawing function in your word-processing program or with specialized visual-thinking software such as Inspiration Software. My vision board, which I have on my computer, is private, easy for me to check in with regularly, and portable, because I can save it on my laptop when I travel. I'm able to import photos, lyrics, videos, music, quotations, poetry, inspiring stories, and research downloaded from the Internet. You might also work with a dry-erase board, doodling and writing on it, and altering its content at will. It may also help to place visual reminders in your car, near your bathroom mirror, by a light switch, or anyplace else where you might stop in the course of your day and meditate for a minute on what this note or symbol means for you.

When you work with your mindfulness journal, you may want to have your vision board in front of you. As I've said, keeping this type of journal and committing to specific, regular times for writing in it builds a system of accountability so that you don't become distracted and stop pursuing your vision. When you have your vision board in front of you, you're reminded of what you need to do. You can focus on overcoming the hindrances that are holding you back while recording new ideas that come to you.

The following template for a vision board can aid you in identifying your visions and steps, as well as the hindrances currently blocking you and how you might remedy them. You can use this in conjunction with your mindfulness journal. Keep in mind that your steps in the process may not be completely linear. At any given time, you may be working on several tasks or projects related to your vision. If so, you may want to cluster tasks so that you can have a map of how you might tackle the challenges before you.

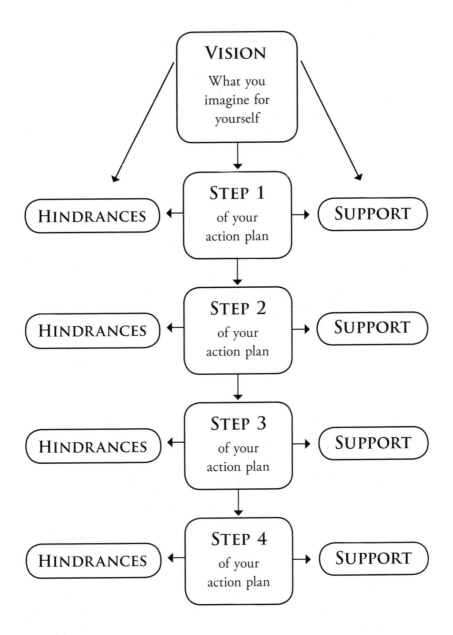

Following is an example of how a woman with children, going through a divorce, might begin sketching out the steps of her vision, identifying and working through hindrances in a nonlinear way (you might have a dozen or so projects related to your visions).

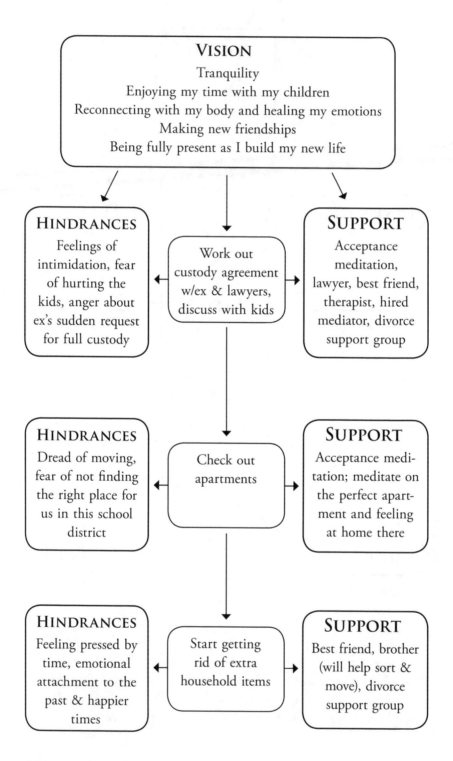

Here's an example of a vision board that someone who's writing a book might create.

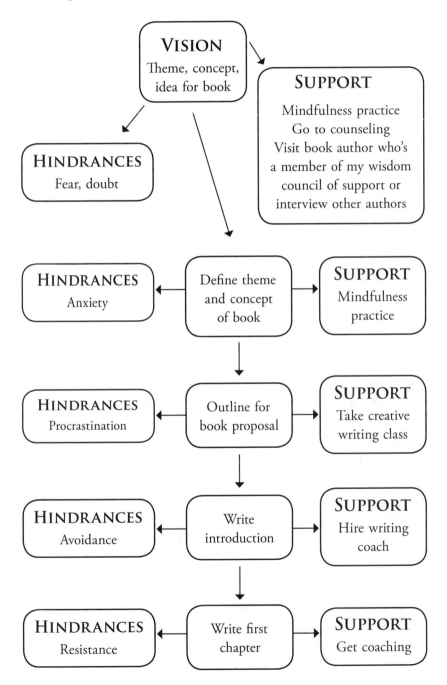

YOUR TIMELINE

The paradox of setting goals is that you want to hold yourself accountable to a timetable to keep yourself on track while maintaining flexibility. The propensity of the mind is to think, talk, and plan too much. This busyness can distract you, but mindfulness will help you engage in fruitful planning, clarifying, refining, and organizing. It'll also help you to be realistic about your time frame for accomplishing any particular task.

In your research, you may learn how long processes take generally, and even discover some specific information. For example, my client who was writing a book learned that it typically takes nine to twelve months from the time a book publisher accepts an author's final draft of a manuscript to when the book is available in stores, but a self-published book can be produced from a manuscript in a matter of weeks. Knowing this, he had to look at all the other considerations: Was it truly an advantage to have the book in his hands that quickly, if it meant not having a publisher distribute it? Could he set up his publicity plans during the short period when the book would be in production? Also, he had to determine how long he was willing to wait to find a literary agent and publisher, given that he could self-publish the book far more quickly. There was no "right" answer to whether he should seek a publisher or self-publish, but to make his decision, he needed to have a realistic idea of how long the various parts of the process would take.

The most difficult aspect of producing that book turned out to be the writing, because he had no clear sense of whether he was taking "too long" to write it and whether the slowness of the process signaled a problem in his plan. Mindful of his anxiety and discomfort over this unpredictable aspect of his plan, he used his observing mind to set aside his unwholesome and unproductive thoughts and feelings, and simply focused on getting his writing and editing done. Having a structured routine reassured him that he was making progress even when it was slow, and mindfulness allowed him to recognize when he needed to take a step back and do more research or learn new skills.

Years ago, a wise mentor taught me about surrendering to a process instead of feeling trapped by time. I was studying psychology at the University of Massachusetts, and whenever I had a very important decision to make, I would go to the house of Buddhist teacher Teresina

Havens. In her seventies at the time, Teresina loved to garden and would prune and plant while listening to my tales of feeling overwhelmed, confused, or frustrated by some challenge. Rather than sit me down and guide me into thinking harder, she'd simply direct me to begin weeding one of her flower beds. I had tremendous respect for her and appreciated her taking so much time with me as we weeded, planted, chopped vegetables for lunch, and interrupted our conversations about my latest woe to note whether the zinnias needed more water or what to add to our salad. But as a type A person, I'd think to myself, "She sure takes forever to talk through something!" After going through this lengthy process with her a few times, it finally dawned on me that she was deliberately slowing down my stream of thoughts and helping me reconnect with my creativity and intuition. She was guiding me in the process of letting the answers unfold from within. A typical school advisor would've spent a half hour talking to me about my application for a particular scholarship, but her slower method allowed me to develop my own ideas about how I would present myself on paper and at the interview. Slowing down and getting in touch with natural rhythms—of growing, eating, and learning—will instill in you patience and flexibility.

ASSESSING YOUR PROGRESS

Figuring out how long it should take to reach your goals can be difficult and can generate anxiety or worry. When you look at your goals and your checklist for manifesting your vision, you may find that your progress isn't as steady or as spectacular as you'd hoped. Because mind-strength enhances optimism, you're less likely to become deeply discouraged and frustrated. You'll be better able to focus on the progress you've made instead of on how far you have to go.

While mindfulness makes it easier to let go of clearly unwholesome or unproductive activities, it can be much harder to assess those that are seemingly wholesome and productive, particularly if they were important parts of your plan in the past or if they seem to be crucial elements in your "winning formula." One of the members of my wisdom council of support was a psychologist who felt he had to develop a platform, a cottage industry of sorts, that would allow him to meet his goal of bringing his ideas to the largest possible audience. His well-researched plan included becoming an author and radio-talk-show personality, and eventually having a live network TV show, as well as teaching workshops and training assistants, traveling, blogging, and continuing to run clinical practice. He was very successful at some of these endeavors but not others—generally, the ones he didn't enjoy. One day, frustrated by an illness he felt was connected to overworking, he asked me for feedback on what he might be doing "wrong." I asked him to tell me what part of his work was making him feel wooden.

He answered, "Having the radio show and running my clinic, but I have to keep doing the show to maintain my audience, and I have to run the clinic to retain my credibility."

We talked at length, and as we did, he started to recognize that while running his clinic had indeed built up his reputation, he no longer needed to do it to have people respect his professional accomplishments. What had once served him so well was holding him back in other ways. We also brainstormed about the radio show, exploring the possibilities, and he realized he could set up his own Internet radio show, broadcasting from his home, and eliminate the feeling that he had to conform to the expectations of the radio syndicator he'd been working with.

It wasn't easy for him to let go of what seemed like crucial pieces of his plan, but he recognized how drained he felt by them and how his old belief that he *had* to have these elements in place just so had prevented him from creating the life he wanted. As he began to simplify his plan and hone his vision, he eliminated other activities and soon felt enlivened. His passion returned, and he began reaching a wider audience and feeling more fulfilled.

No one can tell you how to adjust your plan to make it more fulfilling, but others' honesty and insights can help you find the answers within. Over the years, my wisdom council of support has greatly contributed to my own success, personally and professionally. You may have your own council to rely on, but in the next chapter, you'll discover how to assemble the best possible team of support and how to work with them most productively.

CHAPTER 11

Working with a Wisdom Council of Support

You must have chaos within your soul
to give birth to a dancing star.

—Nietzsche, *Thus Spake Zarathustra*

Your friends, family, or neighbors can offer you practical or emotional support at times, but to come through a crisis and make the biggest breakthroughs in personal transformation, it's best to cast a wide net and draw in support from multiple sources. As you move forward with filling in the details of your mandala and carrying out your plan for creative transformation, I suggest you assemble what I call a "wisdom council of support."

Like an owner assembling a start-up baseball team, you begin with those players who are already available to you, being mindful of the strengths and weaknesses of each. Seeing where you need improvement in your team, you imagine who might fill in the gaps, and launch a search for new team members. As you add appropriate players, enhancing your team, it'll be easier to let go of those who are no longer serving you well. You may retain a relationship with them, but recognizing that you can't rely on them for the type of support you need, you'll stop looking to them for what they can't give you and instead invest in relationships with those who can engage in reciprocal support.

It takes time and concerted effort to process and integrate major losses, and many caring and well-intentioned people may not be able to sustain their support over long periods. This is why it's important to have a wisdom council and also be open to support groups, which have an emotional focus and a mission that includes long-term support.

If you're uncomfortable asking for or receiving help and guidance, keep in mind that every member of your wisdom council will benefit from participating. Every teacher learns from the student, and every master learns from the novice. Peers learn from each other, and elders are inspired by interacting with those who are at an earlier stage of development. Mindstrength will allow you to communicate and interact with your wisdom council members in a wholesome way. You'll be able to find opportunities to reciprocate in your relationship with each council member, making them feel valued and appreciated.

Some people may be able to serve in multiple positions on this council, but it's important to be mindful about the tendency to lean on the same people over and over again in the hope of avoiding the emotional uneasiness that arises when you step out of your comfort zone and meet new people. As the wheel turns, mandalas are swept away by the winds, and new ones must be formed, so be open to finding new members of your wisdom council. Then again, some of your council members will remain close and become special, lifelong advisors.

The core players on your team will fulfill the following roles:

PEER: Most people have several peers they already rely on, whether friends, family members, or colleagues. Peers are approximately at the same point along the road as you are: they're your age or at the same stage of life, career, or development. They can share with you what they've learned so far and compare notes, as well as reassure you that their experiences have been similar, helping you feel less isolated.

EDUCATOR: When facing a crisis or transition, or attempting to create a new mandala for yourself, you need access to individuals who have the skills and knowledge to educate you in key areas where you need training and development. In fact, an educator may inspire you to begin the process of creative transformation even when you're not in the midst of loss, encouraging you to break out of your old ways of operating and try something new. You may or may not need to have a close relationship with an educator, such as a teacher or professor, a motivational speaker, or an expert who shares information with you through workshops, lectures, books, online courses, or professional consulting sessions.

LEADER: Like an educator, a leader may or may not have a close personal relationship with you, but will serve as a role model. A leader's steadfast values, resilience, integrity, vision, and courageous leadership can inspire you and even perhaps help you discover your own leadership potential.

DHARMA TEACHER OR MEDITATION GUIDE: A dharma teacher is a guide to the terrain of inner states of consciousness who is trained in and has used meditation, contemplative prayer, and yoga techniques, and thus can provide expert counsel on this pathway of exploration. Today's Western dharma teacher replaces the model of the Asian roshi, yogi, or guru, merging ancient Eastern systems of knowledge with modern Western models of awakening consciousness.

COACH: A trained and experienced coach can be an invaluable member of your wisdom council of support, assisting you in organizing your ideas, developing a sense of purpose, clarifying your goals, and expanding or paring down your action plan so that you can achieve results.

ELDER: An elder isn't necessarily an older person but someone who's wiser and more experienced than you are in an area you'd like to develop. Due to having had similar experiences to yours, an elder can offer you a perspective you might not have otherwise. An elder is often attuned to rhythms and cycles, and the pacing of projects or life events.

MENTOR: A mentor is a special elder who, like a Zen gardener, is interested both in the process and the outcome, in seeing you achieve results and seeing how you do it. The mentor sets aside his ego's need to be placed on a pedestal, and is eager to watch you rise to your highest potential, even if it means you surpass him in some way. A mentor has an innate, genuine desire to help you expand, grow, and reach your potential, regardless of any benefit to him if you become successful.

THERAPIST: A counselor's aim is to assist you in achieving well-being and healing. To accomplish this, she must honestly confront you and wisely guide you as you come up against hindrances, areas of resistance, and avoidance behaviors. Often, counselors encourage you to explore your childhood, past, and family of origin to understand your patterns. Recognizing that your emotional traumas of the past may have left you hungry for admiration, attunement, attention, clear boundaries, and caring guidance, a wise and skilled psychotherapist can help you over-come self-sabotage and unwholesome feelings of shame and inferiority.

Selecting wisdom council members requires that you be sensitive to others' needs, boundaries, and time. You want them to be available to you, but some members of your council won't be able to be on call, or respond quickly or at length to your requests for guidance, insight, and help in working through problems. Some require pay for their services, while others don't. All will be in a reciprocal relationship with you even if, at times, one of you is giving more than the other.

Mentors and educators play an important role on your council, because they'll help you keep evolving instead of staying locked into old formulas that feel comfortable but hold you back. I've been mentored in clinical psychotherapy for more than thirty years, on and off, and while there are plateaus in my creativity, as well as my teachers', we also make breakthroughs as a result of our supportive relationships, our respective roles in them, and all that we learn from each other. By allowing yourself to be expansive instead of constrictive, and by trusting in the give-and-take of support, you can tolerate plateaus and develop a clear sense of when it's time to move on and collaborate with someone new or stick with your current support, feeling confident that together, you'll break out of the plateau in your relationship.

With any council member, exercise wise speech and mindfulness as you communicate, so that you're both comfortable with the way you interact and what each partner contributes. Also, while you can rely on some members for emotional support, others will be there for you with wisdom and practical advice but won't validate your emotions or encourage you to express and explore them. Be mindful of a peer's need to exchange ideas and facts without bonding over emotions. You have a choice to encourage him to engage in a more emotionally open dynamic with you, replace him with another equally knowledgeable peer, or maintain your relationship with him on his terms, accepting this boundary. A mindful member of your wisdom council may be completely open about her limitations and encourage you to seek support from others to supplement hers.

When you've experienced a major loss, you may feel so lonely and abandoned that you become convinced you have no one to turn to for support. If so, don't avoid this feeling. Be aware of it, remain present with it, and explore it. Sometimes, the feeling of abandonment is real, because your access has been cut off to people who were of great support to you in the past, whether it's a romantic partner you've split from, a friend who died, or a community you had to leave behind. Sometimes, however, what you're actually feeling is the void of the unknown, an emptiness that can feel bottomless. By remaining present with that feeling instead of distracting yourself from it, you can transform it by bringing in its positive qualities. Allow yourself to tap into your core creativity; use the Lone Explorer Meditation in chapter 7 to help you.

Human beings are social creatures. We think of ourselves as separate individuals, when in fact we're intricately intertwined with all beings and all of nature. Just as the frogs in a pond cannot exist without the bacteria and the algae, so we, too, must admit that we all need support from those outside of us. When it's difficult for you to trust that you can and will receive support, and you're resisting the work of assembling or honing your wisdom council of support, you may want to use the following Wise Mentor Meditation to hear your inner wisdom as you experience, if only in your imagination, support and guidance from others.

Wise Mentor Meditation

In the Wise Mentor Meditation, you'll imagine someone providing you with encouragement and wisdom. This could be someone you know or knew, a famous historical figure, or someone you wish to meet. Although the wisdom she imparts may not be true to what the actual person would tell you, the point of this meditation is to access your core inner resources of wisdom and creativity while experiencing emotional support from another.

Begin a mindfulness meditation and, when you're ready, envision yourself in this person's natural environment, seeking counsel as a humble student.

Gaze into your wise mentor's eyes. In them, see acceptance, kindness, and quiet wisdom. Say to your mentor, "I am seeking your counsel, your wisdom, and your creative input."

Imagine your mentor nodding and encouraging your questioning.

Don't tell her your story. Your mentor knows all you've been through, all you've figured out, all your worries and concerns. Simply say, "Please help me. Guide me with your wisdom."

Sit quietly as your wise mentor shares her simple yet deeply insightful advice. Listen carefully to each word.

Feel your wise mentor's support as she laughs and says, "Don't worry so. You'll be able to do as I've advised. You'll know all the steps you must take." Hear this acknowledgment of your own wisdom and strength, and allow your confidence to rise. Sit with your awareness of your strength and wisdom, and relish all the wholesome feelings you begin to feel.

Thank your wise mentor for this helpful counsel.

RESISTANCE TO RECEIVING SUPPORT

Sometimes, we know that it would benefit us to receive support, but we resist accepting it because we feel ashamed, perceiving ourselves as weak or needy. After a loss, we may not snap back as quickly as we thought, and may experience a confusing mix of feelings. An elder who has traveled this road and knows its twists and turns can be of great help, whether it's an older person, someone who has gone through the specific loss we have, or someone who has been through a tremendous loss of his own and recognizes that the path to healing can be quite crooked.

Often, we've internalized expectations of how we should handle crisis and change, and without having questioned these expectations, we become frightened or embarrassed by how different our experience is than what we'd thought it would be. As a result, we may resist the support we need. It's important to work through this resistance as we build mindstrength, and view support as wholesome as we begin building and improving upon our team of supporters. Remember, even highly accomplished people can falter, disappoint others, and fall short of their own expectations. Wise people know this and humbly acknowledge their own limitations, recognizing that each of us is continually healing and evolving.

FINDING NEW COUNCIL MEMBERS

A good way to begin finding new wisdom council members is to ask people you know for recommendations, making sure to ask what it is about this person that your friend, colleague, or therapist values. Your idea of what constitutes a good therapist or educator might be very different from someone else's. You may also want to approach people you have no personal connection to. You might be surprised by who would be willing to offer you support. A client of mine attended a writer's conference and was quite surprised by how freely the experts there, from agents to editors, offered guidance to her as a beginning writer, tailoring their advice to her particular set of goals. Also, someone who seems extremely busy may be willing to carve out time for you. A psychologist friend of mine was raising funds for the creation of an executive health care retreat center, and asked for a meeting with the head of a major communications company. He agreed and later said he'd chosen to meet with her because he'd recently lost a loved one to a disease and had a desire to help others who suffered from the same disease. He became very much involved in this cause, offering not just money and encouragement, but also advice on how to overcome obstacles and achieve the goal of making the retreat center a reality.

As you mindfully observe the potential members of your wisdom council and consider their answers to your questions, recognize that while no one's perfect, your ideal council member will have several important wholesome qualities.

MINDFULNESS: Mindfulness, as you've learned, leads to open-mind creativity. A mindful support member can lead you toward open mind and help you access your own core creativity and inner resources as well as uncover any hidden resistance. A mindful therapist says, "When you were talking just now, that was the first time in a long time I've seen you speak with joy and passion in your voice. Let's explore that." A mindful peer says, "You seem nervous about asking for what you deserve. Why do you think that is?" and works with you to find ways to overcome this obstacle.

REFLECTIVENESS: We're all human and flawed, but a council member who truly doesn't recognize his flaws or limitations won't be able to set them aside to help you. A reflective physician says, "I'm seeing something here that concerns me, and I'd like you to go to one of my colleagues who knows more about this" rather than dismissing your experiences and symptoms. A reflective peer says, "I've been thinking more about what you said the other day, and I realized that my own issues got in the way and prevented me from seeing your situation clearly."

ACCESSIBILITY: Some council members will be able to devote a lot of time to you or respond quickly to your requests, while others will be less accessible. You may be able to supplement their accessibility by using technology to get support elsewhere, for instance, consulting an online support group for people with your specific health problem, or a peer who's part of your professional network, to learn basic information and get some perspective on whether your issue needs addressing immediately or whether your sense of urgency is rooted in anxiety rather than actual need.

CREATIVITY: A creative coach says, "I want you to try a totally different approach to this problem and see what happens. Let's role-play the difficulties you're having in this relationship and see if we can achieve some clarity." A creative peer says, "Have you considered trying this option?" Ideally, this would be someone with core creativity who inspires you to enter a state of open mind.

EMPATHY AND COMPASSION: An empathetic and compassionate elder validates your pain, sadness, and anger, even as he provides perspective and helps you to believe that "this too shall pass." An empathetic peer recognizes your need to talk about your emotions and, even if she can't spare the time you really need, strongly encourages you to get emotional support from other sources as well.

NONREACTIVENESS: If you react with some resistance or defensiveness to the guidance of someone on your wisdom council, it's helpful if that person can be nonreactive in response. A nonreactive coach or therapist doesn't become exasperated when you're slow to make a change you know you need to make, and instead patiently helps you explore your resistance. A nonreactive peer listens to you as you vent angrily, without encouraging you to remain in a state of anger; she'll help you break out of the unwholesome thoughts that led you into an unwholesome emotional state.

STRONG, WHOLESOME VALUES: Members of your wisdom council of support are the most helpful when they're strong but not rigid, grounded in their wholesome, productive beliefs, like a supple tree whose branches sway in the wind without losing their shape or form. Whenever possible, choose council members who share your core values.

CONFIDENCE: A confident council member may confront you, saying, "I know that right now you're scared that you haven't yet found an answer to that particular problem, but I feel that you're compromising your values by settling for the situation you're describing." Every council member should be willing to stand up to you, even when you're being defensive, recalcitrant, or stubborn.

WISDOM: Wisdom is more than knowledge; it's the synthesis of knowledge and perspective. You can't have perspective without knowledge, and knowledge without perspective limits your ability to advise and counsel effectively. A council member should be both skilled and knowledgeable in her area of expertise, as well as wise overall.

OPENNESS TO LEARNING: A council member should be willing to further hone his skills and expand his knowledge at all times to avoid becoming rigid. Ideally, he would have his own wisdom council to consult and the willingness to continuing his education throughout life.

CONTENTMENT AND PASSION: Although seemingly contradictory, these two qualities allow a council member to balance striving with accepting, in order to experience a healthy yearning rather than wanting mind. In his book *It's Not About the Bike* (2000), cyclist Lance Armstrong explained that in his battle with cancer, he needed to be a fierce proponent of his health while being grateful for living, breathing, and eating another day, in order to balance drive with contentment.

Working Effectively with Your Council Members

To be truly supportive, a member of your wisdom council must be willing to challenge you. When your entire support team is comprised of yes-men, you become myopic. It's common for leaders to fall into this trap when they become successful and powerful or famous. Many of the great Zen masters, Tibetan rinpoches, and other wise teachers from Asia who came to the United States during the sixties and seventies fell prey to the hindrances of desire and wanting mind, because they didn't seek help and guidance from their own wisdom councils of support. Today at Spirit Rock, a Buddhist retreat center in Northern California where senior dharma teacher Jack Kornfield is a guiding leader, as well as at many other Zen and Buddhist dharma centers throughout the world, senior teachers use what they call a "council process" to create a system of accountability. The council members sit in a circle, one person speaks at a time while the others listen in silence, and issues such as ethics and teacher conduct are explored. Too often, in groups that have become successful, dialogue about interactions and dynamics shuts down as everyone focuses solely on maintaining success, and egos get out of hand.

If your team members are intimidated by you or in awe of you, or so uncomfortable with conflict that they avoid confronting you when they see that you're not being true to your values and passions, they can't help you. Without honest confrontation from council members, you'll become isolated and unable to see the wider picture of what's happening, what challenges you're facing, and what opportunities are available to you. Exercising wise speech, they can approach you respectfully and speak truths you need to hear.

Council members need to be up to date and aware of what changes are currently taking place, as well as what changes may happen in the future. A sense of vision can give someone incentive to remain creative and open in the face of obstacles, enabling them to keep a sense of perspective as they keep their "eyes on the prize." Again and again, we see sudden shifts in industry and technology that cause traumatic responses in people who resist the tides of change. I witnessed the upheaval in the music industry when, seemingly overnight, computer files became a major form of music distribution and many people who worked at record companies were soon out of a job. Change is inevitable, and a strong council member can help you remain alert to signs of it and assist you in preparing yourself. When working with your council members, ask questions about what they see lying ahead in the road for you. Are there trends or recent developments they're aware of that they can explain to you? Will new technology alter your experience in an unexpected way? If the council member is an elder, ask for his perspective. How did he successfully navigate changes in the past? Did he witness firsthand the reorganization of an industry, or get caught in a sea change when technology or medical advances drastically affected his field? What did he learn from the experience?

To further broaden your perspective, you may want to consult with many people on your council, particularly if you're facing a very challenging situation or weighty decision. Be mindful of your feelings as you consult multiple advisors and listen to their insights and advice.

Keep in mind, too, that each member of your council brings her own perspective that colors her advice and potentially blinds her to certain aspects of the situation while giving her insight into other aspects. If you're concerned about the pacing of your recovery from a loss or how long it'll take to achieve a particular goal, an elder will have more perspective than a peer. Similarly, a peer who knows you extremely well may be able to recognize your hidden resistance, while an elder you don't know quite as well might overlook it.

Having a variety of people on your council giving you contradictory advice is an asset if you can be mindful and grounded in your own intuition and self-awareness. As I said before, when I was inspired to send Mark and Selena, the couple who had lost their children, to an Indian city where they would have to face and experience their emotions over the loss, I consulted many members of my wisdom council and listened to my mind's and body's responses to their feedback. Because my intuition about this idea was so strong, I wasn't swayed by their discouraging words. When I finally had a council member agree with me, it was a mentor who had known me for years. He intuited why I felt so strongly that this was the correct course of action, and I understood why I so strongly resisted the consensus and stuck with my gut instinct.

The longer you work with someone, the more you each can intuit what the other is experiencing. Close friends and long-term advisors can "read" you because they've seen you in many situations over a long stretch, so they have a wider perspective. Sometimes, members of your council can be blindsided by changes you make; for example, I had a client who, after fourteen years of running a business with her husband, decided to move out and completely dismantle the family, which shocked many of her friends. Usually, however, people who've known you for a long time wouldn't be surprised by even a seemingly drastic sudden change—and those who've counseled you and mindfully listened to you would know that such a "sudden" shift was in the making for a long time.

COLLABORATING CREATIVELY

Having members of your wisdom council of support, or other like-minded people, come over and collaborate with you, so you can bounce ideas off each other, is an excellent way to tone yourself creatively. The support of others in a class can increase your discipline, because you have a ritual of attendance at a scheduled class and the support of several people taking it together. A class works best if the instructor uses a basic formula for supportive learning (provided next) that you can adapt whenever you're working with another person to explore ideas. These steps promote vulnerability and openness, and prevent a shutting down of the creative flow. Even if you aren't the leader of a group, you can suggest these ground rules for dialogue in order to steer people away from being so focused on themselves and their emotions that they can't support others in a mindful and caring way, and participate in a productive collaboration.

WISDOM COUNCIL OF SUPPORT

Having members of your wisdom council of support, or other like-minded people, come over and collaborate with you, so you can bounce ideas off each other, is an excellent way to tone yourself creatively.

---

1. *Be mindful and dedicate your full attention to the person who's speaking, performing, or presenting so that the person feels completely supported.* Often, I've been in business meetings where the corporate culture allows for bored body language, whis-

pered asides, and clear indications that people aren't listening. Mindstrength will give you the ability to remain attentive and to speak up with courtesy and honesty when the speaker veers off course and his inner distraction or digression influences others to tune out.

2.   *After a presentation, provide positive responses. If it's appropriate, have everyone applaud or thank the presenter after she's finished. Provide several positive comments before moving into the mode of constructive criticism.* One of the advantages of long-term collaborative relationships is that enough trust is built up that the participants have lowered their defenses and aren't easily hurt by criticism, even when it's given almost immediately after their presentations. In the healthiest brainstorming session, even the most preposterous idea is respected and considered, if only for a few moments. While it may indeed turn out to be completely unworkable, allowing yourself to consider it nonjudgmentally opens you up to a deeper level of creativity, possibly sparking a great idea that wouldn't have come to you otherwise.

3.   *Have members of the group provide constructive criticism and advice, choosing their words mindfully so as to keep the focus on assisting the other person rather than on expressing themselves.* Always remain open to possibility, even as you hone and craft ideas. Allowing yourself to shift into negative emotions or impatience will prevent you from accessing core creativity.

If you feel that the collaboration has become unbalanced and that you're compromising and giving too much, or not getting support for your ideas and desires, mindfully explore with your collaborator why you feel that way. Clarify your expectations and listen to your collaborator describe his. Then, you can mindfully work to find common ground.

SERVING ON SOMEONE ELSE'S COUNCIL OF SUPPORT

Serving on someone else's wisdom council is a way of giving back, but it also helps you better hone your own vision. Often, I become self-reflective after lending support to someone else, asking myself, "Am I applying this counsel in my own life?" This doesn't mean we should be hypercritical, but it's often easier to see in others what we can't observe in ourselves. By developing mindstrength, we find the courage to notice when we're giving advice that we ourselves should heed, and instead of brushing aside our discomfort over that discovery, taking time to explore it. Helping others also helps us recognize our own inner wisdom and compassion, and inspires us to continue developing those attributes.

Once you've embraced your need for support, which is a key to the art of creative transformation, you can move forward into a new mandala, knowing that you're not alone and that if your plan doesn't work out, you'll have the strength to regroup and find the passion, courage, and commitment to start anew.

CHAPTER 12

Accepting the Turn
of the Wheel

Trust your own innate knowing
and the energy moving
within you.
Life speaks to you
through your deepest longing
and guides you with every step.
As soon as you trust yourself,
you will know how to live.

—Goethe, from *Faust*

As the wheel of fortune turns, the section that was in the mud gets dried in the sunlight while the parts that were in the sunlight roll into the mud. Buddhism teaches that happiness is a momentary state of mind, body, and energy, so when you're happy, relish it, but be mindful that the wheel will inevitably turn. Similarly, when you're unhappy, recognize the fleeting nature of your emotions and experiences, learn from them, and know that this too shall pass. Accepting the turn of the wheel brings contentment and helps you trust in the three-step process of creative transformation when it becomes clear that you must design a new mandala. In fact, the mandala is shaped like a wheel to remind us of this ever-rotating wheel of fortune.

If you develop mindstrength and master the art of creative transformation, that wheel will get stuck in the mud less often, and when it does, it'll emerge into the sunlight more quickly. By using the methods for tuning in to your creativity explained in this book, you can reenter open-mind consciousness and stay in touch with the passions that define and shape your vision. Obstacles will seem less daunting, and you'll be better able to accept your circumstances when your vision doesn't work out the way you'd planned.

THE EBB AND THE FLOW

When you're meeting your goals, being productive, feeling a sense of purpose, enjoying prosperity, and flourishing in all areas of your life, it can feel as if you've reached the end of a long road and all suffering is behind you. If you've emerged from a trauma or loss, or a long period of unhappiness, the desire to believe that you've "arrived" is especially powerful. Given that genuine inner happiness fluctuates, it's important to be mindful as you ride on the rim of that ever-turning wheel, rather than hold on to the misconception that life and happiness are static.

Your goal must be to remain open to each moment and what it brings, whether it be positive, neutral, or negative, thereby freeing yourself from distractions, hindrances, and the fleeting desires that create wanting mind. Peaks are wonderful, but they don't last forever, so it's important to drink every drop of juice from the fruit when it's at its height of ripeness, rather than hoard it fearfully or squander it. Otherwise, when you end up in the valley again, you're more likely to experience the suffering caused by wanting mind and wish that you could return to your previous circumstances. Working with people in creative industries, I've seen how the idea that "you're only as good as your last project" creates an unwholesome dissatisfaction and constant striving to do better, a perfectionism that leads to a lack of appreciation for the great triumphs of life. Enjoy the flow, savoring it and allowing yourself to feel sated.

In an ebb period, impatience and doubt inevitably arise. The wanting mind longs to take charge, so it can be hard to accept that you can't control how or when you'll meet your goals. When you feel emotional distress and pain in response to upsetting situations, patience keeps you from being reactive and making poor choices out of frustration. It allows you to be in harmony with the timing of others, who have their own rhythms and may help you to manifest your vision. Mindstrength allows you to be patient and remain present in the moment as your life unfolds before you. It helps you clarify whether circumstances feel right, and whether you're acting in ways that are in accordance with your values and core passions. Often, the first response to the unexpected is resistance and the feeling, "This isn't working," but upon closer examination, you'll realize you're on the right path after all.

To prevent feelings of impatience and anxiety, it's good to set specific, realistic goals for yourself, based on what you've learned about the typical timetable for achieving your goals. However, if your target date arrives, and you realize that for all your hard work, focus, and dedication, you still aren't where you'd planned to be, assess the situation mindfully rather than automatically give up on it. You may need more time to heal from a loss. Perhaps you're very close to a point where a dramatic shift will occur. Mindfulness will give you clarity, allowing you to recognize why your projected timing didn't work out and accept that there were circumstances beyond your control; that you procrastinated, became distracted, or engaged in avoidance behavior; or that you don't have the passion you thought you had. You'll recognize that boredom doesn't necessarily come from a lack of passion. Sometimes it comes from being impatient and from not being mindful of the process and the opportunities for growth that it offers. A mindful musician who spends hours playing scales isn't bored, because he's fully present in the process of building a foundation of skills to support his vision.

Whenever you're in a lull, mindfulness will alert you to the possibilities for learning and growth, and remind you of the larger vision that guides you. Using mindstrength can help you avoid the pitfall of focusing on boredom and the obstacles in your path. There's a wonderful movie called *The Diving Bell and the Butterfly* (2007) that's based on the true story of a man who was left almost completely paralyzed by a stroke. He could communicate only through blinking one eye, and the observer had to patiently recite the alphabet until he blinked, letting her know that she'd hit upon the letter he wanted to convey. Despite this extraordinary hindrance, he recognized that he still had his imagination and was able to use this communication method to write a book he was under contract to write. His memoir would no longer be about his life as a successful magazine publisher (which is what he'd been before the accident), but would instead be about his experience of feeling utterly trapped inside his body. The result was a book—and later, a film—that captured the beauty and art of his dramatically transformed life.

Our rush to get to the next goal often prevents us from discovering the marvelous gifts that patience provides: the ability to let go of restrictive ideas about time and allow creativity to flow through us in its own mysterious rhythm. In the West, we live in a fast-paced world where the goal is to continually move forward and upward. We're uncomfortable with quiet periods, but there are learning rhythms, healing rhythms, and creative rhythms, all of which include ebbs and flows, peaks and valleys. As an artist of life, you'll experience times when you're in creative flow, and times when you're working hard to hone, craft, and manifest your vision.

Recently, I heard an American pundit scoff at the CEOs of the big three automobile manufacturers for driving to Washington in hybrid cars after learning that it looks bad to fly in corporate jets when you're asking the government for a bailout. He complained that the nine hours they would spend driving from Detroit would be a waste and that they could address their companies' problems in that amount of time. A different way of looking at it, one that neither the pundit nor the CEOs probably thought of, is that when we're being reactive, and not clearly thinking through our circumstances or envisioning a breakthrough, nine hours in a car, gazing out at the fields and mountains until we lose track of time and connect with a deeper creativity, can be time spent productively. Our desire to come up with the right solutions, right now, conflicts with the natural rhythms of creativity and blocks us from the more fulfilling and rewarding work of envisioning something greater than merely fixing our problems.

THE DARKEST EBB: DEPRESSION

Sometimes, the ebb of happiness is very low and lasts a very long time. Depression doesn't have to block you from a life of purpose and fulfillment. Both Abraham Lincoln and Winston Churchill suffered from depression, yet neither overly identified with this affliction. They recognized that this "black dog" (as Churchill called it) would appear of its own accord, and they accepted the rhythms inherent in a depressive temperament. I tell depressed or bipolar patients that focusing on why they have this affliction may be useful up to a point but that a far more productive question is, "What now?" We focus on getting the client the proper medications and natural vitamin supplements or hormones, and arranging for emotional support, which alleviates the worst of the depression. Then we explore how the depression or manic energy can be used as fuel for a purposeful life. I often point out that Lincoln allowed himself to feel sadness for himself and for the country, which was embroiled in a brutal civil war, and accessed his compassion. I believe that his experience of often feeling enslaved to his dark moods allowed him to empathize with the suffering of slaves, making him a great and visionary leader who was determined to free them. Churchill was tormented by his depression, and his inner struggle with his mind and moods may have been what allowed him to become an anchor for the British people during their darkest hours. Reaching deep inside himself and discovering his compassion, recognizing that even his most oppressive despair would lift in time, as it always had, he could speak with conviction about hope and courage for a better tomorrow. As he once said, "We shall draw from the heart of suffering itself the means of inspiration and survival."

CATASTROPHIC LOSS

Recently, one of my clients experienced three tremendous losses in a matter of months: her mother died in a freak accident, her husband told her he was gay and no longer wanted to be married, and she was laid off from work. Today, a job loss or health crisis can lead to a devastating domino effect of unemployment, crippling debts, loss of health insurance, stress-related illness, and even homelessness.

An against-the-odds series of crises, catastrophes, and losses too often leads to self-blame. I've seen clients who were overwhelmed by their feelings of guilt and powerlessness after a monumental loss—particularly if they felt they had a great deal of security built up that seemed to protect them from disaster. Such guilt often stems from a defensive need to believe that we have more control over life's events than we truly do. Sometimes, taking a look at others' experiences, or doing a "reality check," can alleviate these feelings at least somewhat. Nearly half of all Americans live paycheck to paycheck with less than five thousand dollars in assets (Scelfo 2008); not knowing that, people often feel that their employment-related crises are signs of personal failure.

Catastrophic losses too often cause people to embrace unwholesome beliefs such as "God is punishing me" or "This must be karma; I must've done something terrible in a previous life." These types of beliefs lead to the question, "Why?" or "How did I cause this?" instead of the healthier questions, "How can I use mindfulness to focus on my immediate experience? What am I thinking, feeling, and sensing now?" After attuning to the now, ask "What's *next*? What do I need to do?" These questions are at the core of creative transformation. We need to look forward, even while embracing the pain of the moment. Rebuilding after any great loss can be extremely difficult, but again and again, I've seen people use mindstrength and the art of creative transformation to pull themselves out of a valley of despair and even create successes they never would've dreamed of before their initial loss. A forward-thinking view can lead to reinvention and healing.

Losses that aren't catastrophic on the surface can nevertheless be experienced as emotionally devastating when they echo an earlier unhealed trauma. One of my clients, David, had recently been jilted by his lover and had withdrawn from all his normal activities, to the point where he was let go from his job because of multiple absences. I knew that we had to get to the core of whatever past emotional trauma had triggered such a severe reaction to the loss of his partner.

David told me that when he was eleven, his parents had divorced, and he'd moved across the country with his mother and siblings to an apartment where he had to share a room with his brother and sister. He felt the loss of his private room, which had been a large sanctuary for him, but I suspected that this was not an overwhelming loss for him. I asked him what was happening in the room as he visualized it, and he said, "My dog's coming into the room, and his tail's wagging."

I asked him what had happened to the dog, and he responded that it had run away, according to his mother. He had always suspected that this was a lie, because his brother had said they weren't allowed to have a dog in their new home and that they couldn't really afford a pet now that his mother was trying to make ends meet on a waitress's salary without child support. Exploring this loss with me in the safe environment of therapy, David revealed that he'd always suspected his mother had actually euthanized his dog. He told me that after that dramatic change in his life, he'd begun to perform poorly in school and become withdrawn. He'd dabbled in drugs and petty crime before joining the military and eventually making his way out to Los Angeles, where he worked a day job and pursued acting.

The River of Time Meditation (which follows) helped me recognize that for David, losing a romantic partner reignited in him powerful feelings of abandonment, loss, and betrayal. In a sense, he'd felt that if his mother could make his beloved pet disappear, and if his father had disappeared as well, he might somehow be rejected and abandoned by his mother too. Recognizing that there was a reason why he was particularly sensitive to this loss helped him overcome his sense of failure and unworthiness, which we worked on in therapy. I had him visualize talking to his dog and expressing how sad he was to have lost him. David became overwhelmed by emotion as he imagined the dog telling him that he would never have left David, and that he still loved him and watched over him.

Shortly after that, David began to get his life back on track, taking up weight lifting and running, and making advances in his acting career. Recognizing the roots of his profound feelings of loss and abandonment had been the first step in healing them.

River of Time Meditation

Begin the process of mindful meditation, and after a time, envision yourself standing alongside a river, the river of your life. The moving waters are your own vitality, or life force, moving forward continually despite all that happens on the riverbank.

Pick a point along the riverbank and walk upstream toward it, moving into the past. This is a place in your life where you experienced a regret, loss, crisis, or trauma. Take a seat on the riverbank, and as you gaze at the passing waters, breathe deeply. Watch yourself go through this past painful event as if you were watching an old home movie. Breathe out the constricted energy that has long held the pain, regret, or trauma inside of your body. Observe as it begins to flow out of you. When this life event has finished unfolding, look into the eyes of your younger self and say, "It's okay.

Everything will be healed downstream, I promise." Reassure your younger self until you feel that the turbulent feelings have calmed. Bid your younger self good-bye, and then turn and walk the other way, downstream, feeling the vital power of the river alongside you.

Experience yourself opening to the future with a fresh and renewed sense of hope and possibility as you move forward, releasing and healing your past. If your internal movie held an old regret, such as never finishing a project that meant a lot to you or dropping out of college in your very last semester, now see yourself picking up where you left off, taking action and finally completing this task. Experience the exhilaration and the wonderful sense of renewal that arises in you as a result.

Observe your healed, future self. Look into the eyes of this future self and ask, "What wisdom can you share with me?"

Listen closely to the answer. Listen as your future self reassures you that you're in the process of healing even now. Feel this self imbue you with courage, strength, and love.

TRUSTING IN THE UNKNOWN AND THE UNEXPECTED

I'd been traveling throughout India for months when I finally arrived at the Mahabodhi temple in Bodh Gaya, India, where the Buddha experienced enlightenment. Hoping for a mystical experience, I began meditating at daybreak. A few hours into my meditation, a realization came to me: "You are already in the opening, in a state of open mind." I felt a dissolving of my personal self and an enormous sense of curiosity as wonder and infinite potential filled me. I was fully present in this blissful experience, ready to take in all the joy and fulfillment that I knew would rush into me, when suddenly, some children came up and threw pebbles at me. They giggled as they teased me and touched my long hair. My focus was broken, and I thought, "Here I am, a breath away from crossing over into this grand experience of the mystical other, and these children are interfering!"

Yet because I was in open mind, I quickly recognized that this experience was part of the opening that we all seek, the connection to core creativity, which leads to breakthroughs we could never imagine in our ordinary minds. I let go of my instant reaction of wanting more, and recognized that I was meant to awaken to joy and playfulness in this moment. I'd been stuck on having a particular experience, but by letting go of my striving for that mystical ideal, I was achieving the real opening: the realization that all is perfect, no matter what the position of that ever-turning wheel of fortune. I opened my eyes and began to tease the children in return, tickling them and enjoying their laughter. My heart remembered that we have to be open to everything as it happens in its own time, or even in divine time rather than in our time.

In creating a mandala, particularly after a loss or crisis, the temptation is to stay focused on the future, on achieving a wholesome state of mind and positive circumstances, but you can't do any of that if you don't surrender to the unknown and the unexpected. Awaken to what's right in front of you, right here and now. This profound opening to your unique essence is where the distinctions of self, other, and the divine blur, and where you merge into that vast oneness.

At every turn of the wheel, we face the challenge to open into joy, bliss, and peace or into pain, sorrow, and agony. We discover that perfection and imperfection are not two separate qualities but one, and that they become our teachers for our growth and awakening. As you find the joy and the lesson in your situation, you'll open up to what you're meant to experience.

In the sweet territory of silence,
we touch the mystery.
It's the place of reflection and contemplation,
and it's the place where we can connect with the deep
knowing,
to the deep wisdom way.

—Angeles Arrien

References

Andriani, L. 2003. The dollars and sense of Suze Orman: How a waitress turned stockbroker combined the heart and the wallet to become America's favorite financial guru. *Publishers Weekly*, February 24, 1-5.

Armstrong, L. 2000. *It's Not About the Bike: My Journey Back to Life*. New York: G. P. Putnam's Sons.

Batchelor, S. 1997. *Buddhism Without Beliefs: A Contemporary Guide to Awakening*. New York: Riverhead Books.

Bennis, W. 1984. *Leadership in America*. Arlington, VA: Soundworks/ Planet Tapes. Audiocassette.

Chopra, D. 1994. *Ageless Body, Timeless Mind: The Quantum Alternative to Growing Old*. New York: Harmony Books.

Cohen, L. 2006. A Thousand Kisses Deep. In *Book of Longing*. New York: HarperCollins Publishers.

Cresswell, J. D., H. F. Myers, S. W. Cole, and M. R. Irwin. 2009. Mindfulness meditation training effects on CD4+ T lymphocytes in HIV-1 infected adults: A small randomized controlled trial. *Brain, Behavior, and Immunity* 23 (2):184–88.

Das, Lama Surya. 1998. *Awakening the Buddha Within: Tibetan Wisdom for the Western World*. New York: Doubleday Religion.

Dass, R. 2007. Personal communication, December 26, in Maui, HI.

Davidson, R. J. 2000. Affective style, psychopathology, and resilience: Brain mechanisms and plasticity. *American Psychologist* 55 (11):1196–1214.

Davidson, R. J., J. Kabat-Zinn, J. Schumacher, M. Rosenkranz, D. Muller, S. F. Santorelli, F. Urbanowski, A. Harrington, K. Bonus, and J. F. Sheridan. 2003. Alterations in brain and immune function produced by mindfulness meditation. *Psychosomatic Medicine* 65 (4):564–70.

Deutschman, A. 2000. *The Second Coming of Steve Jobs.* New York: Broadway Books.

Diving Bell and the Butterfly, The (*Le Scaphandre et le papillon*). 2007. Directed by J. Schnabel. Belgium: Miramax Films and Pathe Renn Productions.

Epstein, M. 1993. Awakening with Prozac: Pharmaceuticals and practice. *Tricycle* 3 (1):30–34.

Evans, D. 1993. Personal, postconcert social communication, August 28, Dublin, Ireland.

Hillman, J. 1997. *The Soul's Code: In Search of Character and Calling.* New York: Grand Central Publishing.

Lazar, S., and D. J. Siegel. 2007. The mindful brain: Reflection and attunement, and the neuroplasticity of mindful practice. Lecture presented at the UCLA Extension and Lifespan Learning Institute's conference on Mindfulness and Psychotherapy, October 7, Los Angeles.

Lazar, S. W., C. E. Kerr, R. H. Wasserman, J. R. Gray, D. N. Greve, M. T. Treadway, M. McGarvey, B. T. Quinn, J. A. Dusek, H. Benson, S. L. Rauch, C. I. Moore, and B. Fischl. 2005. Meditation experience is associated with increased cortical thickness. *NeuroReport* 16 (17):1893–97.

Neruda, P. 1982. La Poesia. In *Isla Negra.* New York: Farrar, Straus, and Giroux.

Maupin, E. 1990. Zen meditation study. In *Altered states of consciousness*, ed. C. Tart. New York: HarperCollins.

Merton, T. 1968. *The Asian Journal of Thomas Merton.* New York: New Directions Publishing Corporation.

Rand, M., and R. Alexander. Mindfulness Based-Somatic Psychotherapy, *USABP Journal,* Fall 2009. Vol 8, #2.

Rossi, E. L. 1993. *The Psychobiology of Mind-Body Healing: New Concepts of Therapeutic Hypnosis.* New York: W. W. Norton and Company.

Scelfo, J. 2008. After the house is gone. *New York Times,* October 22, Home and Garden section.

Segal, Z. V., J. M. G. Williams, and J. D. Teasdale. 2002. *Mindfulness-Based Cognitive Therapy for Depression: A New Approach to Preventing Relapse.* New York: The Guilford Press.

Siegel, D. J. 2007. *The Mindful Brain: Reflection and Attunement in the Cultivation of Well-Being.* New York: W. W. Norton and Company.

Simkin, J. S. 1976. *Gestalt Therapy Mini-Lectures.* Millbrae, CA: Celestial Arts.

Whyte, D. 1992. Statue of Buddha. In *Fire in the Earth.* Langley, WA: Many Rivers Press.

Wilber, K. 2007. *The Integral Vision: A Very Short Introduction to the Revolutionary Integral Approach to Life, God, the Universe, and Everything.* Boston: Shambhala Publications.

Williams, M., J. Teasdale, Z. Segal, and J. Kabat-Zinn. 2007. *The Mindful Way Through Depression: Freeing Yourself from Chronic Unhappiness.* New York: The Guilford Press.

Ronald A. Alexander, Ph.D., is a psychotherapist, leadership consultant, and clinical trainer. He is also director of the Open Mind Training Institute in Santa Monica, CA, an organization that offers personal and professional training programs in integrative mind/body therapies, transformational leadership, and mindfulness.

A leading pioneer in somatic psychotherapy, holistic psychology, mindfulness, leadership coaching, and integrative and behavioral medicine, Alexander conducts professional and personal trainings throughout the United States and internationally. He is an extension faculty member at the University of California, Los Angeles and an adjunct faculty member at both Pacifica Graduate Institute and Pepperdine University. Alexander is an associate member of the American Psychological Association, a clinical member of The California Association of Marriage and Family Therapists, and a diplomate in professional psychotherapy at The International Academy of Behavioral Medicine, Counseling, and Psychotherapy and The American Psychotherapy Association.

Foreword writer **Lama Surya Das** is a leading Buddhist teacher, founder of the Dzogchen Meditation Center, and author of Awakening the Buddha Within and many other books and articles. For more than ten years, he has written the Ask the Lama column at www.beliefnet.com.

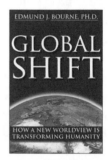